Samuel Train

Indians and pioneers

An historical reader for the young

Samuel Train

Indians and pioneers
An historical reader for the young

ISBN/EAN: 9783337727376

Printed in Europe, USA, Canada, Australia, Japan

Cover: Foto ©ninafisch / pixelio.de

More available books at **www.hansebooks.com**

INDIANS AND PIONEERS

AN HISTORICAL READER FOR THE YOUNG

BY

BLANCHE E. HAZARD

Teacher of History, High School, Concord, Mass.

EDITED BY

SAMUEL T. DUTTON

Superintendent of Schools, Brookline, Mass.

ILLUSTRATED

THE MOI

GLADLY AND GRATEFULLY

DEDICATED

TO

Albert Bushnell Hart,

WHOSE INTEREST IN STUDENTS OF
AMERICAN HISTORY
EXTENDS FROM HIS CLASSES AT
HARVARD UNIVERSITY
TO THE YOUNG CHILDREN FOR WHOM
THIS BOOK IS INTENDED.

AUTHOR'S PREFACE.

THE aim in writing for young readers these stories of "Indians and Pioneers," or "Earliest Days in America," has been to treat the history of America simply and briefly, yet with the regard for accuracy and the care in selection of material which are necessary in order to set forth the truth.

Two features in these stories are introduced, in the confident hope that they will be found both interesting and practical; one is the study of the glacial and rough stone periods, which is, of late, made more attractive and intelligible to young readers, because taught through "simplified mineralogy" and clay-modeling; the other feature is the large use of quotations from the sources, giving the original wording and quaint spelling of the narratives of the European pioneers to America.

To the little band of "child critics," who have listened to all these stories while still in MS. form, and who have been frank and helpful in their confessions and suggestions, the author owes many thanks.

At the Peabody Museum and the Harvard University Library, where most of the research work has been done for these stories, much kindness has been shown and generous aid given.

To Prof. Hart, through whose kindness these privileges have come to her, the author owes her chief inspiration in this work.

Acknowledgments are due to Messrs. Houghton, Mifflin & Co., for the use of valuable cuts.

BLANCHE E. HAZARD.

EDITOR'S PREFACE.

The enrichment of courses of study for children is best accomplished by improving the nutritive quality of the intellectual diet of early years. The processes of assimilation and growth go on together. The mind is to be fed and nurtured as well as the body, if there is to be hardy growth and full development.

Applying this principle to the teaching of history, it will readily be seen that the courses of a few years since, devoid as they were of historical material, left the young mind hungry and unnourished. There was nothing in its experience to awaken a taste or create a desire for history. The large mass of children passed out of the public schools with no interest in the history of their own or other nations. Stories, many of them unwholesome and harmful, became their mental pabulum. Even to-day one often finds an even layer of dust upon the works of history in our public libraries. This defect in education is gradually being corrected. Excellent work has already been done in adapting history to youthful needs.

The author of this volume has for the first time told the story of primitive man in America in such a manner as to enlist the interest of any one who has learned to read. Her description of the rude customs and simple habits of the early people of America cannot fail to arouse interest both in the teacher and the pupil. The pictorial representations of their tools and implements add much to the work.

In treating the Indian, as well as the early discoverers and explorers, the author has held closely to the best authorities, and has avoided the stale and hackneyed style which has too often characterized such stories. By means of this and succeeding volumes, it is intended to provide a course of historical reading that shall be valuable alike in the home and in the school.

Only a word need be said concerning method. It is plain that the narrative of history is to be acquired by *reading*. If possible, each pupil should have a book, yet good results are attained when a portion of the class listens to the reading. The teacher's ability to so illumine the narrative as to make it *real*, and to give it not only human but social import, will largely determine the usefulness of this study. SAMUEL T. DUTTON.

INDEX.

	PAGE
Abinos, of Indians	66
Adze (illustrated)	21
Albany, founded by the Dutch	234-235
Named by English	247
Antiquarians, careful work of	11
Ideas concerning glacial men	21, 22
Ideas concerning shell-heaps	39
Antiquities, discovery of	11
Arizona, Cliff Dwellers in	44
Arrow head, found in mounds	36
(see chipped implements)	
Axe, use of by Glacial Men	20, 21
Use of by Mound-builders	36
Balboa	127
Baltimore, Lord, attempts colony at Avalon	162
Instructions to colonists	163
Deposed	165
Bi-ans-wah, story of	71, 72
Blackstone, John	205
Blaxton (see Blackstone).	
Boston, capital of Massachusetts Bay colony	193, 202, 206
Early names of	205-206
Fortification of	206, 208
Map of	207
Prosperity of	215-217
Bradford, Wm., ruling elder	109, 177
Journal of	179-183, 186-187, 190
Brewster, Wm., Puritan elder	172, 174
Brooklyn	235
Burial mounds, description of	34, 41-42
Contents of	34-35, 39
Cabot, John, birth of	113
Theories of	113
Sets sail March, 1497	114
Relations of, to Henry VII	114
Landfall of	114
Second voyage of	116
Cambridge	202, 220, 221
Cannonicus	225
Cape Cod, reached by Pilgrims	177, 179
Explored by Pilgrims	180-183
Carolina (see North Carolina and South Carolina).	
Cartier, Jacques, settlements attempted by	126, 127
Carver, John	174-175, 177, 190
Cathay, search for by way of the West	93
Cave Men, Time of	30
Possibly descendants of Midden men	31

	PAGE
Caves used as dwellings	30
Contents of	30-31
Salt Cave of Kentucky	31
Central America, early migrations from	53-55
Visited by Columbus	109
Champlain, settlements made by	126
Charlestown, founding of	202
Charlton (see Charlestown).	
Chipped Implements, location (illustrated)	12
Of prehistoric people	13
Found in glacial deposits	19-20
Made by man	20
(Illustrated)	20, 21, 25
Uses of	21
Use of (illustrated)	25
Of Indians	77
Cliff Dwellers, habitation of	44, 46
Habits of	46, 47
Ancestors of	53-55
Cliff Dwellings, location of	46
As cities of refuge	46
Description of	46
Coddington, William	225, 227
Collections in museums of prehistoric implements	13
Largest and finest	13
Explained by custodians	13
Colorado, Cliff Dwellers in	44
Colonists, Spanish	99, 106, 128
French	126-127
English	129, 138
Dutch	230, 251
Swedish	251
Columbus, Christopher, birth of	96
Education of	96
Among books	96
Great aim of	96-97
Helped by Ferdinand and Isabella	96-97
Diego, son of	97
Making preparations at Palos	97
Helped by Pinzon brothers	97
Ships of	97
Sets sail August 3, 1492	97
First voyage of	98
First landfall of	99
Builds Fort La Navidad	99
Letter to Santangel	99-101
Received at Spanish court	101
Second voyage of	104
Sets sail September, 1494	104
Builds the town Isabella	104

INDEX

	PAGE
Columbus, treatment of savages.	104
Blamed by colonists	106
Third voyage of	107
Sets sail May, 1498	107
Touches mainland of South America	107
Sent to Spain in chains	107
Petitions to the king	107
Fourth voyage of	109
Sets sail May, 1502	109
Touches the coast of Central America	109
In deep distress	109–110
Death of, in 1506	110
Character of	111
Significance of the discoveries of	111, 127
Connecticut, colony of	220, 221
Coronado	127
Cortez	127, 128
Cotton, John	206, 224
Cuba, discovered by Columbus	99
Dale, Sir Thomas, High Marshal of Virginia	149
Makes strict laws	150
"Dale's Code"	150
Dare, Virginia	138–139
Davenport, John	222
De la War, Gov	148–149
Delaware	251
Dishes (see Pottery).	
Dorchester	202, 220, 221
Drake	128
Drift, left by glaciers	17
Scattered over country	17
(Illustrated)	18
Dutch, in Connecticut	220
Claim to discovery of the region of the Hudson	231–233
Relation with the Indians	240
Indian attacks on	241–242
Conquest of, by English	246, 251
In Pennsylvania	257
Dutch East India Company send out Hudson	230–231
Dutch West India Company chartered	234
Send out colonists	235
Letter of P. Schagen to	236–237
Establish Patroon system	237
Receive complaint from colonists	242–243
Called to account by Dutch government	243
Duty-boy, in Virginia	158
East Indian trade in Europe, influence of crusades upon	90–92
Destroyed by Turks	92
Search for western passage in order to continue	93
Eaton, Theophilus	222, 223

	PAGE
Endicott, John, leadership of	196–197
Finns	257
Fire-buckets	8–10
Florida, shell-heaps in	28–29
Fort Orange (see Albany).	
Fox, George	254, 255
Freemen, in Massachusetts	200–201
Free-willers	157
Friends (see Quakers).	
Frobisher	128
Frosty Stone, story of	22–27
Genoa, birthplace of Columbus	96
Birthplace of John Cabot	113
Geography, early ideas of	89–90
Studied by Columbus	96
Of America in 16th century	121
Germans	257
Gilbert	128, 138
Glacial age, climate of	14
Conditions of, existing in Alaska and Greenland to-day	14
A story about	22–27
Glacier Men, name of earliest people	14
Tools of	19
Life of	20
Occupations of	20
Flee from advancing ice-sheet	21
Original home of	21
History of	21
Descendants of	22
Glaciers, formation of	14
(Illustrated)	15
Extent of	16
Motion of	16
Path of	16
Deposits made by	16–17
Dissolution of	17
Gloucester	217
Gravel banks, cut through for railroads	12
Guanahani, Discovered by Columbus	99
Guilford	222
Hakluyt, Richard	128, 135
Hartford	221
Hawkins	128
Hayti (see Hispaniola).	
Higginson, Francis	198
Hispaniola, discovered and named by Columbus	99
Described by Columbus	101
Mining in	104
Hudson, Henry, explorations for the Dutch	230–231
Hutchinson, Anne	225
Ice Age, The (see Glacial Age).	
Ice Boy, The	22–27
Indiana, mounds of	32
Indians, origin of name	14
Pueblo (see Pueblo Indians).	

INDEX.

	PAGE
Indians, discovery of	56
Other names of	56
Ancestors of	56
Influence of Europeans upon	56–57, 59, 80
Trading by	57
Manufactures of	57
Primitive customs of	57
Appearance of	58–62
Dress of	58–62
Dress of (illustrated)	61
Kinship of	63
Villages of	64
Customs of	64, 67, 69, 72, 73, 77, 78, 81, 82, 83, 84–85, 87–88
Wigwams of	64–66, 85
Village of (illustrated)	65
Abinos of	66
Children of	69–75
Games of	71, 80–82
Characteristics of	71
Love for children of	71–72
Education of	73–78, 82, 83
Quintans of	75
Canoes of	77
Weapons of	77
Hunting and fishing by	77, 78, 86
Food of	78, 80, 81
As warriors	82–83, 84
Enlisting of	82
War-dances of	83–84
On the war-path	84, 85
Head-dress of	85
Girls and women	85
Agriculture of	85
Pottery of	86, 87
Embroidery of	86–87
Burials of	87–88
Welcome Columbus and the Pioneers	106
Ill treated by colonists	106, 130–134
Raid Jamestown	148
Massacre Virginia colonists	160
Welcome the Pilgrims	188
Taught to plant Indian corn	189
Relations with Roger Williams	224
Relations with Coddington	225, 227
Relations with Dutch	240
Attack the Dutch	241–240
Treatment by Penn	256–257, 260–261
Interpretation of Feuds, impermanency of	14
Jamestown, settlement of	140
Government of	141
Common-store system of	142
Trouble at	142, 143, 146
Indian name of	145
Reinforced	146–147, 184
Change in government	147
Condition of	148

	PAGE
Jamestown, abandonment of common-store system	149, 155
Ruin of	160
Jersey City	235, 241
Josselyn, John	228
Kentucky, mounds of	32
Salt Cave in	31
Kieft, Governor	244
Knife, made of slate by Moundbuilders	37
La Navidad, fort built by Columbus	99
Found in ruins	104
Long Island, English settlers upon	244
Dutch settlements upon	248
Description of	248–249
Lyford, John	190–191
Maine, described by Josselyn	228–229
Settlement of	229
Union with Massachusetts	229
Mammoths, name of	19
Skeletons of, found near glaciers	19
(Illustrated)	19
Manhattan, origin of name	233
Settlement of	234–235
Purchase of	236
Government of	235
Marblehead	217
Maryland, origin of name	163
Granted to Lord Baltimore	163
Religious toleration in	164–165
Mason, John	228
Massachusetts, attractions in	210–211
Commerce of	215–227
Departure of colonists from	220–221
Massachusetts Bay Company, chartered	196
Servants of	197
Growth of	199–202
Massachusetts Bay Company, Transfer of government to America	200–201
Dependence of civil rights upon Religious views	204
Refusal to surrender charter	218–219
Massasoit, visit of	188
Treaty with the Pilgrims	189
Maverick, Samuel	205
Meadford (see Medford).	
Medford	202
Merchant-Adventurers, Pilgrims sent by	175
Laborers sent by	177
End of business relations with Pilgrims	191
Mesa, description of	49
Mey, Cornelius Jacobson	235
Miantinoma	225

INDEX.

Midden-men, The, origin of name. 28
 Time of.................... 30
 Possible ancestors of Cave Men 31
 Contemporaries............ 44
 Ancestors of , ...53-55
Middens, where found........... 28
 Contents of................ 43
Middle Pitt, story of........... 40-33
Milford 222
Minuit, Peter................... 235
Missouri, Mounds of............ 32
Moraines, Medial (illustrated)... 15
 Formation of............... 16
 (Illustrated)............... 18
Mortar and pestle, found in mounds...................... 37
 Public; in boulders......... 38
Mound-builders, time of........ 32
 Descendants of............. 40
 Child of, a................. 40
 Food of.................... 43
 Contemporaries of.......... 44
 Ancestors of............ 53-55
Mounds, cut through for railroads 12
 Location of................ 32
 Hidden by forests.......... 32
 Great Serpent (illustrated).. 32
 Discovery of............... 32
 Preservation of............ 32
 Shapes of.................. 32
 Uses of.................... 34
 Opened in sections......... 32
 Discovery of. 40
Mound village, a description of.. 34
 (Illustrated).............. 35
 Diagram of................. 41
 Fortification of........... 42
Mount Wollaston................ 205
Nantasket...................... 205
Naumkeag (see Salem).
Netherlands, Pilgrims in 173
New Amsterdam, settlement..... 236
 Growth of..... ...... 238-239, 247
 Religious liberty in....... 238
 Indian raids upon........241-242
 Condition in 1647.......... 245
 Conquest of by the English... 246
 Named by the English...... 247
 Description of............. 249
 Commercial relations with New England................ 250
 Return to Dutch rule....... 250
New Hampshire, settlement of..227-228
New Haven, settlement of....... 222
 Government of............. 222
 A commercial colony....... 223
New Jersey..................... 251
New Mexico, Cliff Dwellers in.... 44
New Netherlands, attractions of.. 231, 233-234

New Netherlands, patroonships in 237
 Suffers from Indian raids 242
 Conquest of by English..... 246
 Named by English 247
 Return to Dutch rule....... 250
Newport........................ 227
Newport, Capt............141, 145, 147
Newtown (see Cambridge).
New York City (see New Amsterdam.
Nichols, Col................... 247
Noddle's Island 205
Norumbega, ideas of............ 121
Norsemen, meaning of the name Viking 112
 Home of................... 112
 Early voyages of........112-113
North Carolina, earliest settlement in..................... 165
 Granted by Charles II...... 166
 Settlers of................ 166
 Trouble in................. 166
Ohio, ancient earthworks in....32, 35
Oholase, an Indian queen......60-62
Oldham, John................190-191
Painting, of Indians............ 62
Patroon system................ 237
Penn, William, secured grant of "lower counties"............ 251
 English surroundings of...253-255
 Land scheme of............ 256
 Treatment of Indians......256-257, 260-261
 Arrival in America........258-259
 Troubles of.............261-262
Pennsylvania, granted and named....................255-256
 Emigration to......... 256, 259
 Native resources of......259-260
 Character of settlers....... 260
 Made a royal province..... 262
Philadelphia, "Quaker City"..257, 262
 Laying out of............. 258
 Rapid growth of........... 259
 Schools of................ 260
Pilgrims, early home at Scrooby. 169
 Religious views............ 170
 Hard times in Holland....171-172
 Ask for help............... 174
 Origin of name............ 176
 Leave Holland............. 176
 Land near Cape Cod........ 177
 Signed the "Mayflower Compact"..................... 177
 Landing of................ 185
 First visit from Indians.... 188
 Privations of the first winter. 190
 Second company of......... 190
 End of common-store system. 191
 Co-partnership, notice of..191-192
 Special mission of........... 193

INDEX.

	PAGE
Pioneers (see Christopher Columbus).	
(See Norsemen).	
(See John Cabot).	
Attracted to New World	120, 122
Achievements of	127
Motives of	135, 136, 137
At Salem	196
In Connecticut	220-223
In Rhode Island	223-227
Dutch	230-239
Pizarro	127, 128
Playthings of glacier child	25
Of Mound-builders' children	41-43
Of Pueblos	53
Of Indians	71-73
Plymouth, site of	184
Origin of name	184
Chosen by exploring party from *Mayflower*	184-185
Laying out of	185-186-187
Growth of	193
Incorporated in Massachusetts colony	193
Pocahontas, Story of her visit to Jamestown	151-154
Becomes Lady Rebecca	154
Polished stone implements, where found	22
Of the Mound-builders, described	36-37
Uses described	36-37
Portsmouth, settlement of	225-227
Pottery, soapstone, found in mounds	38
Clay, found in mounds	38
Found by farmers	39
Decorated by Mound-builders	39-40
Of Mound-builders (illustrated)	42-43
Of the Pueblos	49
Baking of Pueblos	52-53
Comparison of primitive	55
Of Indians	57, 87
Powhatan, storehouse of	67-68
Friendliness	143, 151
Kindness to Captain John Smith	145-146
Reconciliation of	151-154
Prehistoric Springtime, effects on glaciers	17
Life during	19
Prisoner Servants, in Virginia	158-159
Providence, founding of	223-224
Pueblo Indians, ancestors of	50
Deterioration of	50
Spanish influence upon	50-51
Religion of	51-53, 127
Pueblos, habitation of	47
Origin of name	47

	PAGE
Pueblos, dwellings of	47-49
Time of	47
Descendants of	47
Village of (illustrated)	48
Government of	49
Life of	50
Pottery of	50
Ancestors of	53-55
Puritans, religious views of	170, 195, 198, 203-204, 217
Persecution of	195
Charter of	196
Congregational church of	203-204
Dependence of civil rights upon religious views of	204
Early writings of	209-210
Quakers, persecution of, in New England	205
In New Jersey and Delaware	251
Religious views of	253-254, 255
Settlements of	255
Quintans, of Indians	75-77
(Illustrated)	76
Raleigh, Sir Walter, English colonies sent by	138
Redemptioners	157, 238
Religion of the Mound-builders	42
Of the Pueblos	51-52, 127
Discovery for the sake of	122, 132
Introduced among Indians	135
Puritan	169-171, 203-204, 217
Rhode Island, settlement upon	225, 227
Purchased from Indians	225-227
Roanoke Island, settlement at destroyed	138-139
Robinson, John, minister of Pilgrims	170, 171
Death of	193
Rocksbury (see Roxbury).	
Roughstone Men (see Glacial Men).	
Roxbury	202
Salem, pioneers at	196-197
Church at	197-199
Troubles at	199-200, 221
Salt Cave of Kentucky, description of	31
Contents of	31
Samoset	188
San Salvador, discovered and named by Columbus	99
Santangel, letter of Columbus to	99
Schagen, Peter, letter of	236-237
Scotch-Irish	257
Sea of Darkness, ideas about	93-95
(Illustrated)	94
Separatists, religious views	170
Persecuted in England	171
Flight of, to Holland	171
Condition of, in Amsterdam and Leyden	171-172-173

INDEX.

	PAGE
Separatists ask for help	174
Sent to America by merchant adventurers	175
Serpent Mound Park (Illustrated)	33
Shawmut	205
Shell-heaps, where found	28
(Illustrated)	29
Description of	28
Contents of	29-30
Age of	29-30
Slavery, introduced into Virginia	156
Smith, Capt. John, disciplined	141
Made president	143
Relations with Indians	144-145
Character of	143-144
Visits Powhatan	145-146
Departure of	148
In Massachusetts Bay	184
South Carolina, earliest settlement in	165
Granted by Charles II	166
Settlement at Charlestown	166
Settlers of	166
Trouble in	166
Spaniards among the Pueblos	50-51
Conquer Mexico, Peru, and Brazil	118
As colonists under Columbus	99-106
Relations with the Dutch	231-233
Squanto, Relations with Pilgrims	189
Stamford	222
Standish, Myles, friend of Pilgrims	172, 177
Chosen captain	187
St. Augustine, settled by Spaniards	128
Stuyvesant, Peter	245, 246
Swedes	251, 257
Tattooing of Indians	62-63
Tennessee, mound villages in	41
Titus description of	53
Tools (see implements).	
Totems, use of	63-64
(Illustrated)	63
Turf Hut, A (Illustrated)	23
Description of	24-25
Threatened by ice-sheet	26-27
Utah, Cliff Dwellers in	44
Van Twiller, Wouter	244

	PAGE
Venice, early merchant sailors of	93
Early home of John Cabot	113
Verrazano, early life of	124
Commissioned by Francis I.	125
Touches North American coast	125
Description of America	126
Vespucci, Amerigo, birth of	117
Interest of, in Columbus	117
Touches South America	117
Fame of	118
New World named for him	118, 127
Virginia in 1618	60
Indian name of	67
English name of	138
Settlement by the English	138
General assembly of, established	155
Life in	155-156
Virginia Company, formed	140
Orders of	144
New charter given to	147
Dealings with Pilgrims	174-175
Walloons	235
War-dances of Indians	83
Watertown	202, 220-221
Weathersfield	221
Weymouth	205
White, John	138
White, Peregrine	179
Wigwams, of Indians	64-66
Williams, Roger, sent away from Massachusetts	204
Founds Providence	223, 224
Arrival of in America	223
Religious views of	223-224
Windsor	221
Wingfield, President, made first president of Virginia	141
In disgrace	146
Winthrop, John, arrival of	199
Election of, as governor	201
Removes to Boston	206
Letter of, to wife	211-214
Statue of	212
Joined by family	214-215
Wisconsin, Mounds of	32
Zuni, Pueblo of (illustrated)	48
Religious ceremonies at	51-52

INTRODUCTORY.

STORIES FROM AN ATTIC.

Did any one ever hear of a boy or girl who does not like to spend rainy days in an attic? There is a large family of brothers and sisters and cousins, in a certain city, who have for their play-room the attic of a big, old-fashioned house that was built before the Revolution. It is full of heavy oaken chests and hair-cloth trunks and mysterious boxes of all sorts of shapes and sizes.

Sometimes grandmother comes up to tell the children who owned these ancient boxes, and where they have been in travels around the world. If the dear granny does not feel able to mount the stairs, over which the children scamper nimbly, she gives the bunch of keys, on their faded green ribbon, to the oldest girl.

The oldest girl is proud of grandmother's confidence, and tries to make the others have an extra good time when she unlocks the trunks and brings out the old bonnets and dresses, the fans and slippers of years and years ago. Once in a while the oldest boy is allowed to take a screw-driver and open some of the chests which belonged to his grandfather, who was a famous friend of the Indians, and a good fighter, too, in his day. From his chests come forth Indian bows and arrows, leather stockings and moccasins, queer pipes, knives, belts, and many things of which the boys and girls do not know the names. Another man in the family was captain of a ship that sailed the eastern seas many years before the children were born.

These young folks used to like nothing better than to be alone among these treasures; not that they wished to be away from grandmother; but it was "such fun" to guess what aunt the horse-hair bonnet fitted; who gave great-grandfather the set of conch-shell buttons that are like a set owned by General Washington. Every one of the boys has his idea of great-grandfather's strength from his big, clumsy musket and his holster pistol, which hang from the rafters.

There was a great mystery for a long time over four long leather buckets, painted red, with great-grandfather's name in white letters. The buckets were half-full of balls, as heavy as lead and old, broken pewter spoons, some of them hammered out flat and thin. One day the mystery was cleared by Aunt Betsey. The children did not ask her. That would have spoiled half the fun, they thought; but one of them heard her tell a visitor that the family still had her grandfather's water-buckets. Every man in the village, she said, was obliged to have one or two sets of water-buckets, and to use them, too, whenever a neighbor's house or barn took fire. Auntie had often heard her grandfather tell how on an alarm of fire all the men of the village rushed out with their buckets and formed two lines between the fire and the nearest well. They kept the full buckets going toward the fire, and the empty ones toward the well just as fast as the neighbors and their hired men could handle them.

"Our buckets are full of bullets and old metal," auntie continued. "I have heard my mother tell how every old spoon and scrap of pewter was saved and hammered out to be melted up and run into bullet-moulds. She said we must always keep that scrap in the buckets, for it is just as it was when the family were at work on it, and the alarm came that Indians were coming and everything was hidden up the chimney."

The children talked this over with the buckets in front of them, and decided that the true stories about the things in the attic were more exciting than guesses and make-believe stories. So, now, they ask grandmother and Aunt Betsey and every one they know for the true stories. Sometimes they are told to look at pictures and read books on our early history and the manners and customs; sometimes they are told to go to museums. They like to do so, now that they have learned that these things show how the people looked and what they did, and even what they were thinking of when the important events happened that the school histories mention.

Of course, these children soon wanted to know about the Indians. Then they asked where the Indians came from; what was this country before there were any attics and old chests, before there were any villages or fire-buckets; what was it as far back as any one knows?

INDIANS AND PIONEERS.

CHAPTER I.

THE EARLIEST TIMES WE KNOW OF.

Of late years people have found many true stories of the men and women who lived in our country thousands of years before our great-grandfathers. The people who have found these stories are called *antiquarians*, which is a long, dull-sounding name to you, if you do not know the meaning of it, and what interesting things are discovered by the hard work of such persons.

STONES HIDDEN IN THE EARTH.

How have they learned such wonderful things, do you suppose? By digging in the earth; by digging in certain places, where they have learned to look for *antiquities*—another word that must be known to be appreciated. Many places where such things lay hidden were first found by accident, by workmen digging wells, ploughing fields, or laying the foundations of railroads, cutting through mounds and gravel banks, and even in old river beds.

GOOD WORK OF ANTIQUARIANS.

The workmen often found curious things, which some antiquarian would hear of, and go hundreds of miles to see.

"Why," he would say, "these workmen have

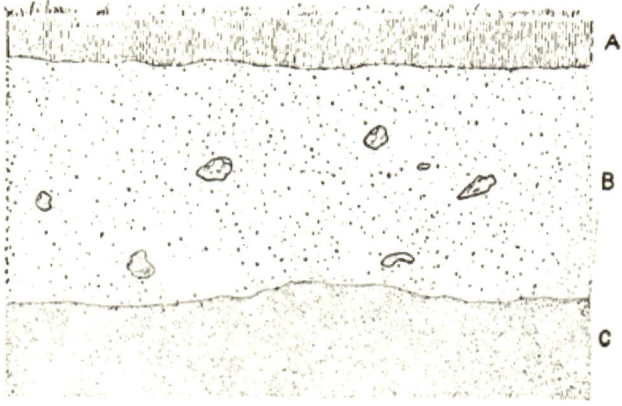

A Black top soil.
B—Yellow drift (Glacial sand) containing chipped implements and flakes.
C- Yellowish-white sand.

come upon things that were made before the time of Indians we know about." The men thought they were cutting through natural earth, but the antiquarian knew better than that. He looked carefully at the outside of the place, and at others like it near by.

Then he brought educated and skilful workmen of his own to open some of them. They worked carefully, so as to see just how the hills or pits were made, and what they contained.

They said: "These stone implements and bones are the remains of ancient people, who must have lived and died and been forgotten before the time of any people known to our histories of America."

That is why these discoveries are called prehistoric.

After the first findings, they began to search for others. Colleges and historical societies, and even the United States government, gave men and money to the search.

COLLECTIONS IN MUSEUMS.

There are several museums where you can see such "finds," all nicely labeled, and oftentimes a custodian to explain to you about them. The largest and finest collections are at the Peabody Museum in Cambridge, Mass., the American Museum of Natural History at Central Park, New York City, at the Smithsonian or National Museum in Washington, D. C., and the American Museum of Natural History at the University of Pennsylvania.

We may not believe all the antiquarians think

about the earliest people. Perhaps by the time you are grown men and women many new discoveries will change their beliefs; but the present discoveries tell us a great deal which cannot be changed. We know that many, many generations of people lived here long before the time of the savages found by Europeans near the beginning of the seventeenth century. The Europeans, who thought this country was part of India, called the savages Indians. They had to have some name for them, so we must have some names for the prehistoric peoples. We call the first people of which we have traces by the name of glacier men.

THE GLACIAL OR ICE AGE.

This is the name for a time in the history of North America when the climate was much more moist and cold than it is now. It was so cold that the moisture fell to the earth in the form of snow. The snows fell continually; and as there were no "warm spells" or any summers to make them melt and run off, they piled up, like the snowdrifts of many winters, one upon another. Then almost all of our country looked as parts of Alaska and Greenland do to-day. All the valleys and hollows were filled with tightly-packed and hard-frozen snow, which we call glaciers. They extended for

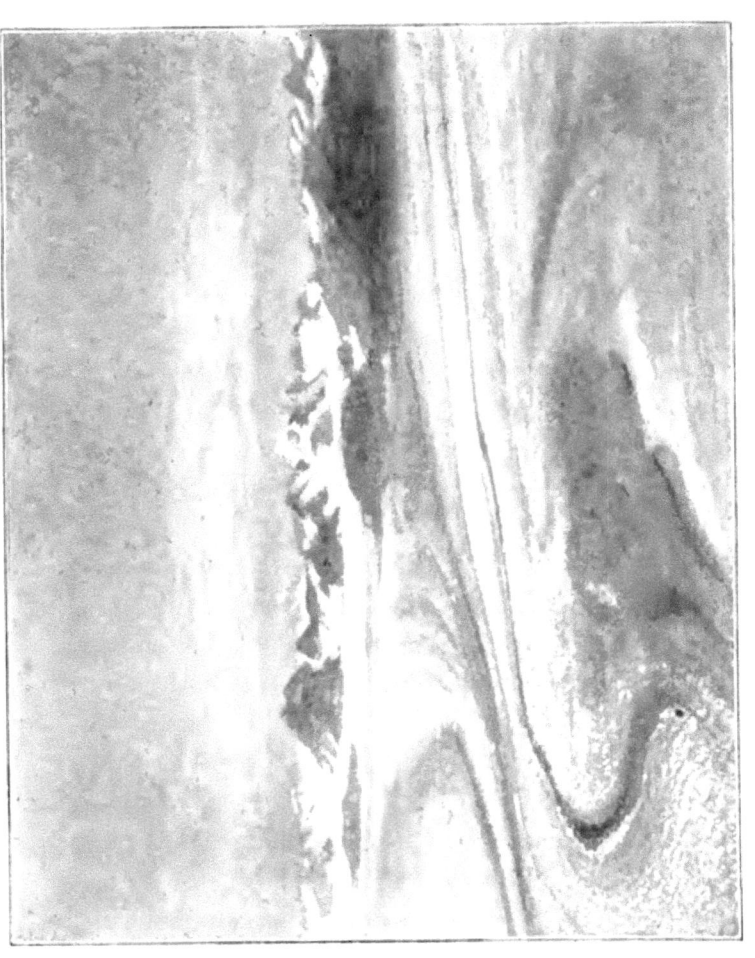

BIRD'S-EYE VIEW OF THE EASTERN PORTION OF MUIR GLACIER, ALASKA.

Showing about 25 square miles. The dark lines are medial moraines. The dark mass in the foreground is a mountain top, which deflects the ice which is moving past it. The ice is doubtless more than a thousand feet thick over most of the area exposed. Photographed by Prof. H. F. Reid. Photo. loaned by Prof. G. F. Wright.

miles and miles in great, broad, white rivers, between the highest mountains. All the smaller hills were covered. All these rivers moved, not dashingly or rapidly, as rivers of water do, but slowly, grindingly, carrying everything they could tear from the mountain sides with them.

If you had been on any of those vast snow-streams, and had driven a row of stakes in a straight line almost anywhere, you would have found, after a time, that your line had grown crooked, or had become an arc, because the middle of the glacier moved faster than its sides. The glaciers moved so slowly that you could not tell that they moved at all, except in some such way as by the stakes. They moved faster in summer, when the hot sun melted them a little, than in winter, and faster in the daytime than at night.

MORAINES.

As the glaciers moved, they carried trees, all the loose gravel and stones of the mountain sides, even big boulders, weighing hundreds of tons. These lay in long rows along the centre and at the sides of the glacier. They are called moraines.

When you roll a big snowball, you know how it takes up dirt, pebbles, and almost everything in its way. Sometimes, after your ball has melted, you find a little heap of the things it picked up. Perhaps, also, there is a broken line of pebbles along the path where you rolled it. The paths of our glaciers have been traced in much the same way.

THE GREAT PREHISTORIC SPRINGTIME.

After a long ice age, when glaciers covered much of our country, a change came in the climate, which we might call the great prehistoric springtime. The air grew warmer, and the moisture fell in rain instead of snow. Then the air grew drier. The rain ceased part of the time. The glaciers began to melt, to crack, to break up, to rush through their valleys, and sail off into the ocean in icebergs. Water rushed from under them in torrents, cutting its way through the valleys and forming deep river channels to the ocean. Wherever the snow melted it dropped its stones, as your snowballs do. Much of our country is still covered with what is called the drift of the glaciers —and very stony farms it makes, too.

Pieces of rock, worn smooth by their travels, are still strewn over the glacial valley, some of them thousands of miles from their native beds, out of which they were roughly pulled in the cold ice age. Laborers often find them far in the ground, sometimes fifteen feet deep, under layers and lay-

A TRAIN OF BOULDERS IN SOUTH DAKOTA.
This is part of a moraine on a prairie. Photographed by Prof. J. E. Todd. Photo. loaned by Prof. G. F. Wright.

ers of dirt and soil that must have gathered during many centuries.

MAMMOTHS.

We think that there must have been animals even as early as then, by the skeletons found near

MAMMOTH.

remains of glaciers. Because these skeletons are so much larger than any animals of our times, we call them mammoths.

THE GLACIAL MEN.

All this time you have been wondering, probably, if there were any people living among the glaciers or in the great springtime. Apparently there were; for roughly-shaped stone tools have been found in some of the layers of the soil covering the deeply-buried glacial boulders. Whenever you hear the word tool, you think of a man to use it. There 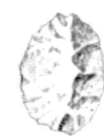must have been men not only to use but to make these things. Rough and odd as they are, some people must have made them; for it is hardly possible that they were worn into these shapes by the action of water and gravel moving over them.

CHIPPED IMPLEMENT OF EARLY MAN. KNIFE.

Men who have studied the natural and artificial shapes of stones, point out to us how these are chipped off in one place, hollowed in another, and smoothed

KNIFE (OREGON).

in another, all in such fashion as to make them useful. Besides, others like them have been found in other parts of this country and in Europe, where there were several proofs that they were made by men of an early age.

LIFE OF THE GLACIAL PEOPLE.

The climate of the country about the ice-sheets was not too cold for trees to grow, or even for a rough sort of farming, people think; for some of the tools found are like axes and hoes. Here are pictures of such stone tools, showing how like tools are used with wooden handles by modern Indians. If they tell a peaceful story of sowing and harvesting, they also tell of trouble. Many times they have been found helter-skelter, as if left in haste. It is thought that they were dropped by men who fled before the advancing ice-sheet, when it began to melt fast, or that they were overtaken by it and killed.

ADZE BLADE OF STONE.

You may see some of these things in the museum collections. They are odd, rough, stone things that would have no meaning to you if you did not know the stories of the people who used them. Some of them seem to have been made to kill animals, some to cut them up for food, others to remove the skin and to make it into clothes. You see we know very little about the people of the ice age. We believe they were here, because we have found tools, like those of a prehistoric people in Europe. Perhaps all were of one race, and our glacial men came from Europe on an ice-sheet which may have spread over the far north Atlantic. There is no proof of how they came or what became of them. Some antiquarians think that they all perished as the mammoths did. Others think that they went north, as the glaciers began to melt, keeping close to the ice-sheet. They believe the

ADZE, WITH MODERN HANDLE, TO SHOW HOW THE BLADE WAS PROBABLY USED.

glacial men's descendants still live in the far north, and are what we call the Eskimos. Still others believe that the rough stone men, as they are sometimes called, grew more refined as time went on, and that it was their descendants who made better implements of polished stone and flint, which we find now by digging in heaps of sand and shells by the water, by hunting in caves, or by delving into large mounds piled up high, in other parts of the country.

FROSTY STONE, THE ICE BOY: A STORY.

Percy Brownley sat up in bed, rubbing his eyes and calling to his mother to come to him quickly. While he waited almost breathlessly for her to step across the hall to his bedside, he looked about his room as if in search of something entirely different from what he saw with his frightened, staring eyes.

His mother's voice seemed to calm him somewhat as she hurried to him, saying, "What makes you shiver so, and what makes you look so frightened, my boy?"

"I guess any boy would shiver and be scared, too, if he were an ice boy, living right near a lot of icebergs that might slide over him in the night. I thought one had, but—but here I am in my own

A TURF HUT

room and not in a turf hut, and I can see the sunlight and the maple-trees—outside my window. I don't understand it all."

"Why, Percy, you have been dreaming—"

"Dreaming? and it isn't true?"

"Why, no! don't shiver so—here—lie down in bed again—pull up the clothes about you, and mother will sit beside you to hear the dream. Now, my little ice boy, tell me who you were in your dream; the son of an ice man?"

"Why, yes! that is just what I was; but not our kind of an ice man. My father was one of the ice men who lived in the glacial time that sister Lucy was talking about with the young professor who came from college with brother Ned, last evening. I was listening to them when you called me to go to bed."

"Then I suppose you went to dreamland to find out more about those people."

By this time Percy was calm and warm. With one hand resting in his mother's and the other free to make gestures, he told her how he had been living in the ice age of America.

"My name was Frosty Stone. I had two brothers and a sister, and I had, why I had a different father and mother from you and papa Brownley. We lived in a hut made of turf, with skins hung

EARLIEST DAYS IN AMERICA. 25

on the inside of the walls. It was dark, and the oil we burned smelt badly. We had wood to burn to keep us warm, but not much, for it was so hard to get. We had to take a long journey of several days to a place where some tall, weather-beaten trees grew. These we hacked down with heavy stone axes. The men used large ones and we boys had smaller ones. On our way home with the wood on our sleds, we went through a settlement where they had corn-fields in summer. Once father got some of their corn, paid for it with his outer fur coat. He thought the weather had changed and he should not need it; but as we neared home, each day grew colder, and he wanted it again. Mother seemed delighted with the corn. She pounded it with a stone and stirred it up with water. I don't believe I should want to eat any of it now, but it tasted good when I was Frosty Stone.

RUDE CHIPPED IMPLEMENT OF EARLY MAN.

RUDE AXE, HAFTED CHIPPED IMPLEMENT. MODERN INDIAN.

"Mother had to make father another coat out of the skin of a deer he shot the next day. She cut the skin off from the fat and flesh with a flat, sharp-edged stone, punched holes in it, and sewed it with such a queer needle. It was coarse and long, made of a piece of thin bone with a big hole for the eye. Guess what she had for a thread, Mamma Brownley! why, the dried muscles of some animals father had killed at different times.

"We had some of the deer-meat cooked on a stone before the fire that night, and felt glad father had to have the new coat."

Then Percy's mother said, "I should think you had a very happy life, and plenty of snow for sliding and snow-balling."

"I think I have had enough. It seemed pretty good for a while, but I was afraid of the great big animals that lived down in the forest region and sometimes strayed up near where we lived, and oh, mother!" exclaimed Percy, shivering again, "the iceberg was so near. It moved towards us a little every day in what we called the summer months, when for a while there was no snow about our hut. Father and Mother Stone used to talk about it, and say they must make another hut farther away from the edge of the ice-sheet. But colder weather came again, freezing it up too hard to move more than a wee speck each day—and then they thought it safe to stay. But oh, one night, after a few warmer days, there was a sudden thaw! We heard it cracking! I thought the whole glacier was coming right over our hut to bury us under the snow, and then —"

"Then you awoke"—put in his mother's calm voice.

"Yes, and found I wasn't Frosty Stone, the ice boy, any longer."

CHAPTER II.

STORIES FROM MOUNDS.

AFTER the people of the ice age, there were several races, or, perhaps, several branches of one race, who covered much of our northern continent. One may have followed another, or all may have lived at the same time. At any rate, they lived differently. If one came before another, the first were probably

THE MIDDEN MEN.

The people who are named after the heaps of refuse and shells they made in the places where they lived, are called midden men. These middens, or shell-heaps, are found on the northwest coast, and along the Atlantic shore, from Florida to Labrador. Some are found also inland along the great lakes and the St. Lawrence River. The old shell-heaps down in Florida are particularly interesting.

Try to imagine great sand or earth-covered piles of mollusk-shells, sometimes joined together so as to form one long line of embankment. Scattered through them are many odd-looking bone tools, and many other strange objects made of the bones of such animals as the elk, deer, beaver and

FLORIDA SHELL-HEAP WORN AWAY BY THE RIVER.
A—Skull in place.
Cut loaned by Peabody Museum.

seal. Remember that only a few of these animals are found now in our country south of Maine and Michigan, and that the heaps are found as far south as Florida. There are some rude cooking-dishes and a few pieces of broken pottery in these refuse heaps, just as you find pieces of crockery in an old ash-heap now.

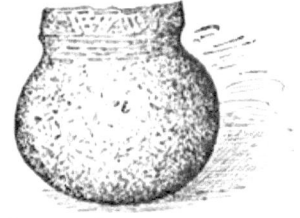

POTTERY VESSEL FROM SHELL-HEAP.

The wisest antiquarians do not know how old these heaps are. They believe that they are not as old as the glacial and early stone age, because no mammoth bones are in them.

From some things they appear very old. Others belong to a later time. So the midden men seem to have lived for many, many years—perhaps many hundreds of years. They seem to have thrown about everything they had into their heaps. In some of the heaps are articles, or pieces of articles, which must have been made in Europe. It is believed that the midden men were not all gone before the early discoverers began to come from Europe, near the beginning of the sixteenth century.

THE CAVE MEN.

Some time during the midden men's period, or after them, lived the cave men. Caves have always been used as dwellings. Even now, in lonely parts of the shores of Scotland, men, women and children live huddled together in dark and dirty caves.

WOVEN SANDAL FROM A CAVE IN KENTUCKY.

Imagine what life in such a place would be; not attractive, or perhaps endurable, for us, yet we find something very interesting about the old caves inhabited many hundreds of years ago. There are caves in all parts of the country that show many positive traces of the people who have lived there.

One of the greatest is the Salt Cave of Kentucky. The rock has been hollowed out partly by nature and partly by the people. Scattered about in the dingy darkness were forms of animals, tools of stone, pottery, and the cinders of several hearths, where they had fire for warmth and cooking. There were pieces of cloth, too. The people wore sandals, and used bags of rope or twine which they made of hempen fibre and the inner bark of certain trees. You may see all these things at the Peabody Museum in Cambridge. Thus you see that the cave men had ropes to fasten sticks for wooden handles to their stone and bone hoes, as is done to-day by the savages about the Papuan Gulf.

WOVEN BAG FROM CAVE IN KENTUCKY.

These things seem like the work of people who knew more than the midden men. Perhaps some of the midden men's sons and their families began to be cave-dwellers before others left off making shell-heaps.

THE MOUND-BUILDERS.

Still another people, called mound-builders, lived in the time of the midden men and the cave-dwellers, or after them. Boys and girls may still see some of their mounds in Ohio, Indiana, Missouri, Wisconsin, and other parts of the country. For centuries they lay unknown and hidden by forests. They were discovered as the lands were cleared, and, fortunately, many of them were preserved. From a distance they look like toy or artificial hills made in circles, squares, rectangles and crosses. The most interesting ones are shaped like animals. In Kentucky there is an immense mound which looks somewhat like the shape of a bear. It measures about one hundred and five feet from the tip of the nose to the tail. In Ohio there is a serpent with open jaws and gracefully coiled tail. When they were first found men dug them up carelessly and ignorantly, breaking and upsetting all that was inside.

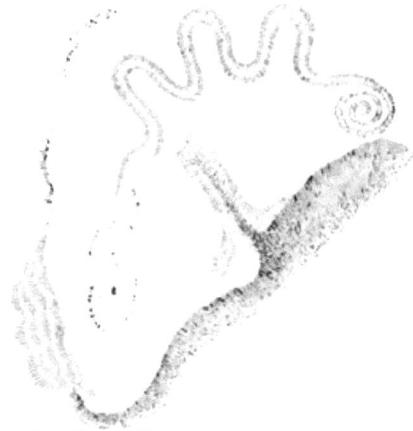

BIRD'S EYE VIEW OF THE GREAT SERPENT MOUND, ADAMS COUNTY, OHIO.

Others, who knew their value, cut into them carefully, so as to open them by sections, keeping

SERPENT MOUND PARK, ADAMS COUNTY, OHIO.
A—Ground line. B—Skeleton in place.
Photo. loaned by Peabody Museum.

everything in place as nearly as possible, to see the contents and the form in which they were built. By this time hundreds of mounds have been opened. The smallest of them seem to have been mere watch or signal mounds. Others were certainly burial places.

MOUND VILLAGES.

The largest of all the mounds seem to have been earthworks for a fortified village. They sometimes formed three sides of an enclosure fronting on a lake or river. Within the limits of these enclosures you may still see scores and scores of pits, where huts and wigwams once stood, the dwellings and workshops, perhaps, of the people who mounted guards in war times on the smallest mounds round about, and buried their dead in the others.

THE BURIAL MOUNDS.

These contained the skeletons of men, women and children. Sometimes these had been carefully placed on flat boulders; sometimes in graves made of flat stones. In one mound the skeletons lay in rows; in another in a circle, with heads toward the middle, like spokes in a wheel. Weapons were often found near the bones of the arm; ornaments of stone and bone lay about the heads, and necklaces made of the teeth of large animals. Vessels of clay seem to have been placed over the graves, probably with food. Savages still put food instead

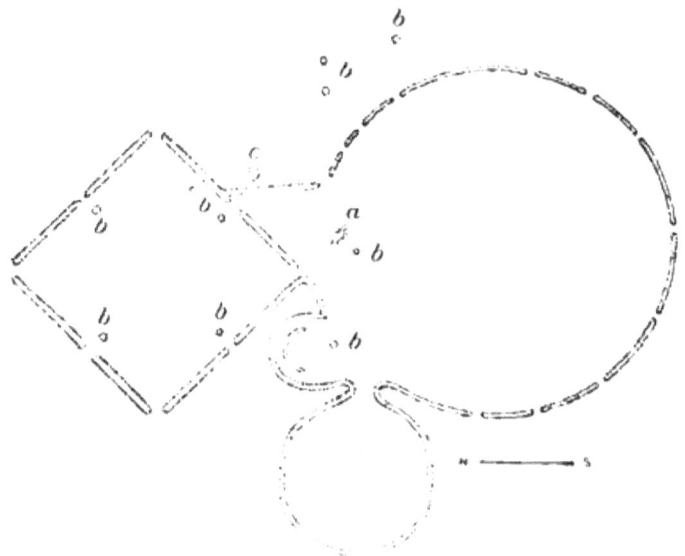

BIRD'S-EYE VIEW OF ANCIENT EARTHWORKS, ROSS COUNTY, OHIO.

a — Large mound containing enclosure of timbers, altars, skeletons and implements, and ornaments of copper, bone and stone.
b b b — Small mounds.
c — Small circular earthwork.
The larger circular enclosure has an area of about forty acres.
The square enclosure has an area of about twenty-seven acres.
The smaller circular enclosure is about eight hundred feet in diameter.

of flowers at the graves of their dead. Ashes near by show signs of the feasts held by the relatives at the grave.

HOW DID THEY LIVE?

To imagine how these different peoples lived, we must look at their tools. They have left a large

STONE AXE.
stone, which you might call an axe, with grooves in it, where a piece of hide or rope may have fastened it to a handle of wood. Other stones, about two and three-fourth inches long, seem like little axes. They are all well shaped, with good edges. Perhaps the children worked or played with the small ones. They seem to have left more arrow-points than anything else. These are of many shapes and of

HAFTED STONE AXE. MODERN INDIAN.

many kinds of stone, especially of what we call
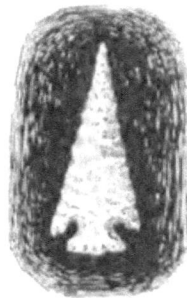
FLINT ARROW HEAD.
flint. Some are shaped like leaves. Others are triangles. These early people had stone knives, to skin animals, probably, and to split bark from trees. Perhaps the women did this work, as Eskimo women do now. Hard and dirty work it must have been; but their hands were protected somewhat from the sharp stone blade by a back or handle of wood. This had holes in it, through which thongs of hide fastened

it to the blade. This shape was most common in the North. In other parts of the country knives were shaped like large arrow-points, and fastened into sticks for handles.

SLATE KNIFE (NEW ENGLAND).

After the skinning of an animal they used its flesh for food, and its fat for various purposes, and stretched and rubbed the hide until it was soft and pliable.

SLATE KNIFE WITH MODERN HANDLE (ALASKA).

When it was properly tanned they bored holes in it with bone awls, and sewed it into rough garments, with the sinews of animals for thread. They may have sewed also with a kind of "Indian hemp," which we call dog-bane or milkweed; for they often used this hemp to make fish lines and nets. Of bone, also, they made different ornaments and tools.

The men probably did the fighting, the hunting and fishing. Flat and notched stones, which look like hoes, and many

SMALL MORTAR AND PESTLE.

mortars and pestles make us think that grain was raised for food also; but there is nothing to show whether the men or the women did the work.

CIVILIZED PEOPLE.

They must have been civilized in many respects. They had large mortars made in boulders and placed in the centre of the town. These were probably a sort of town-mill, for the use of all. Many

Mortar made in a Boulder.
Cut loaned by Peabody Museum.

small ones were found in different places, which seem to have been owned by private families. The smallest ones were used, we think, to grind paint, which was used, perhaps, to ornament the people's faces, certainly to decorate their dishes and vases. These people made dishes of clay and of soapstone for cooking and for many other purposes. They are of various shapes and sizes.

Farmers all through this great country plough up bits of their pottery every year. Some pieces are large enough to show the shape and decorations of the vessel. These tell that the people's houses may have been scattered all over the country; but only in the burial mounds and

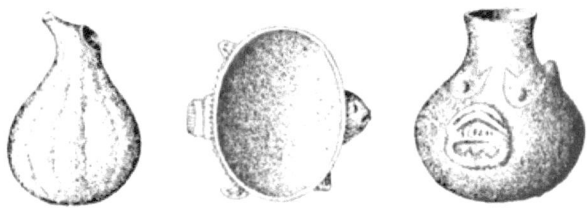

POTTERY FROM ANCIENT BURIAL MOUNDS.
Vessel in form of gourd.
Bowl in form of fish.
Jar in form of grotesque head.

graves are the things found whole. There they have laid, safe from the plough-share for several hundreds of years. We may be more interested in these vessels than in any of the other things, for they tell us more of the people. They tell us how skilful the mound-builders were with their hands, what fancies worked in their brains. Some of the vases are so beautifully designed, so perfectly formed, and so artistically colored, that many archaeologists and ethnologists believe that the mound-builders were far more civilized than any of the natives found in North America by Europeans after the discovery by Columbus. The natives of the seventeenth century may have been descendants of the skilful mound-builders; they may have lived in the same places, gradually neglecting their arts and allowing their hands to lose their cunning.

The natives found by the first explorers from Europe, several generations after them, chased their game through the forests without knowing that the hills they crossed were mounds, and without even a tradition of the early people who built them.

The white settlers from New England, who drove the savages westward and cut down the trees, found the mounds not very long ago. So it is only lately that men interested in prehistoric people have known of them, and begun to trace the stories of those who built them.

MIDDIE PITT, A LITTLE GIRL MOUND-BUILDER.

The grave of a mound-builder's little girl was found one day, by a man who dug into one of those small, round pits, where it is supposed that the people's huts stood. It was in the Lebanon settlement in Tennessee. Below the bottom of the pit the little girl's bones were found on a smoothly-paved grave, with two flat stones at the head and the foot. Beside her were her toys. There were

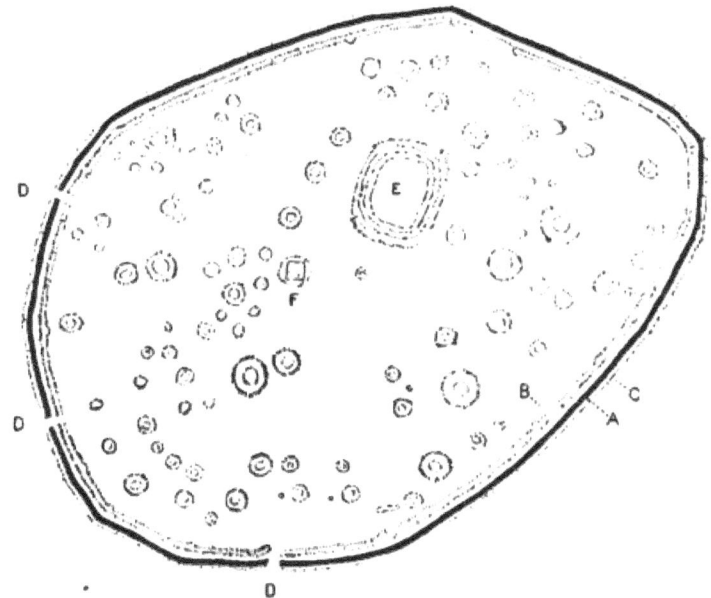

BIRD'S-EYE VIEW OF ANCIENT VILLAGE SITE OF THE MOUND BUILDERS, LEBANON, TENNESSEE.

A—Ditch enclosing village.
B—Inner embankment.
C—Outer embankment.
D—Entrance to village.
E—Great mound. Probable site of council house or important building.
F—Burial mound, with stone graves.
The circular earthworks not designated by letters are probably the sites of dwellings.

some shell beads, pearls and pretty little polished stones, a small earthen pot, a duck-shaped dish, and a water jar, like a bear, with a smoke-stack on his back.

The little girl was fond of these dishes, probably, and her mother filled them with food and water to be buried with her. The mother may have be-

BIRD-SHAPED BOWL (TENNESSEE).

lieved that the little girl needed something to eat and drink, on her long journey to her new home; or she may have believed that bad spirits would eat the food and leave the little girl in peace.

She lived in a settlement of people who had round huts, clustered together within a high bank, which protected them from beasts and made it harder for enemies to get into their village. In the centre of this town was a sort of mound where they had an altar and worshiped their heathen gods. Then there was a large mound used for a burying-ground for grown people. They got the dirt for these big

EARTHENWARE VESSEL (TENNESSEE).

mounds from a place near the wall at one end of their village, out of which they dug so much that it was a big hollow or sink. There the little children could play—I wonder if one of their games was hide and seek! Whatever they played, they came in hungry at noon. What do you suppose they had to eat? We have learned some of the things from the waste heaps or middens that have been found near the pits where their huts stood, much like those of the midden men. The mound-builders left piles of shells of different kinds of mollusks, and bones of various animals and birds. They had plenty of turkey, for they were wild and plentiful all over the country then.

We think that they had mush or porridge, too, made of some kind

BEAR-SHAPED VASE (TENNESSEE).

of grain, probably corn, and cooked over the fire. In the waste heaps are broken dishes that have been smoked and burnt. Perhaps the little girl had her mush every evening out of the duck bowl. At night she lay on some rushes or leaves for a bed and had a deer skin over her. We do not know her name, but I like to call her Middie Pitt.

CHAPTER III.

EARLY PEOPLE OF THE SOUTH-WEST.

While the midden men, the cave men and mound-builders lived in the eastern part of North America, a more skilful people occupied the vast square now covered by the four states of New Mexico, Colorado, Arizona and Utah.

THE CLIFF DWELLERS

lived in many places throughout this region, but where, we do not know exactly. The ruins of their homes are still standing near the rivers Rio Grande, Gila, and branches of the Colorado. Now-a-days travelers find some of that country so hot and dry that they can scarcely endure the climate long enough to look at the wonderful scenery, the great masses of bare rock with deep chasms called cañons, where torrents of water rush through in the short, rainy season. There is more than scenery to admire. High up in the clefts of these wild, bare rocks, are many half-ruined villages, built by a people who have left us almost no other traces of their history.

RUINED CLIFF DWELLING, CAÑON DE CHILLY.

How did they get there? Why did they live there? What sort of people were they? Did they run up and down these sheer cliffs, like a cat on a tree, to visit the rest of the world? Did they have rope ladders, or did they have nothing but the risky hold for hands and feet, which is now afforded by the small notches cut in the face of the bare rocks? From a distance these oddly-shaped notches look like mere natural breaks in the rock; but people believe that they were cut by the cliff dwellers. If they could cut these holes and build such houses, why did they not build stairs up the cliffs? Probably because these dwellings were cities of refuge for a people who lived and had their farms on the plains below. They may have been a war-like people among themselves, or they may have had bitter enemies, from whom they fled to their cliff dwellings so swiftly that the enemies did not know what became of them, for the villages are so like the rocks in structure and in color that they cannot be seen at a great distance.

They were built by a strong and skilful people. Certain parts of the houses seemed to have been watch-towers placed to command a wide view over the surrounding country. There we imagine sentinels watched for the approach of their enemies from the north and west.

From their high places of refuge, the people may have seen the enemy enter the valley below them, where the fields seem to have been under cultivation, and destroy all their homes and farms. Perhaps they always lived in the cliffs and had only their fields below. Certainly they could not have grown anything on the bare rocks.

THE PUEBLOS.

Another ancient people who lived in the southwest were the Pueblos. They were found by the Spaniards and called by a Spanish word which means village. The word is used for the people, their houses and their villages. In fact, a pueblo house was often like a village or a portion of a village. Over a hundred families sometimes lived under the same roof, or, rather, above the same foundation. No one knows how many centuries ago some of these houses were built. Many of them, partly in ruins, are standing now, and are the homes of the descendants of those who built them.

The Pueblos' houses were built in a sort of semicircle or in a rectangle about an open court, from which one story rose after another in terraces like an ancient amphitheatre or the tiers of seats about a modern baseball field. The rooms about the court were but one story high. Behind them

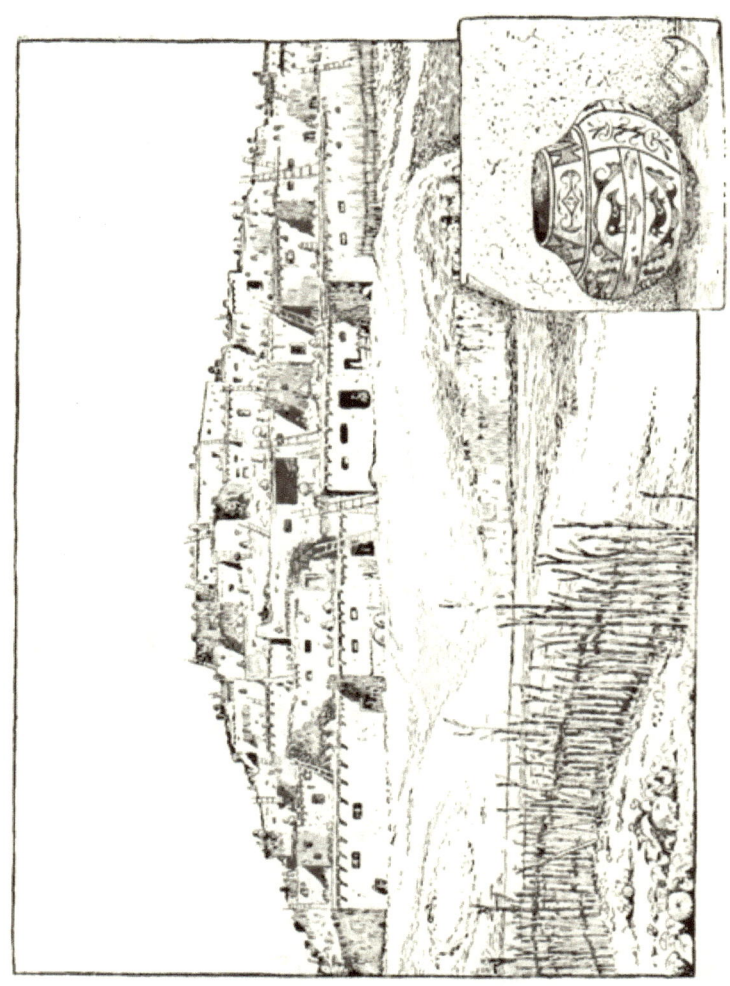

Modern Pueblo, Zuñi, N. M.   Zuñi Pottery.

rose another, and behind them another, till the back of the house was sometimes six stories high.

The lower rooms appear to have had no doors or windows for either light or people to enter from without; but in the floor of each second story room there was a trap-door or scuttle-hole into the room beneath. The lower rooms were used as cellars for storing grain and other food. Each family probably controlled the cellar below its living room. The roofs were made of logs, with brush and bark laid over them, and a top-coating of mud several inches thick. There were no stairs in any part of the pueblos. Ladders were usually left standing on every roof or terrace, so that people could go from one to another till they reached the apartment they wanted. At sign of the coming of an enemy, though, all ladders were quickly pulled up.

THE HEAD OF THE HOUSE.

All the people in one of these great house-towns as they have been called, were sometimes united under the command of one chief or priest. He directed them in building the house, in tilling the fields on the "mesa," as they called the table-land on which the house stood, and in all their work, their religion and their daily life. They may have been a people with many arts. Their farms were watered by canals. Their crops were large. They were warlike, and they successfully defended their villages from their more savage neighbors. They made pottery of more beautiful form, coloring and design than the mound-builders.

PUEBLO INDIANS.

We call the people who live there now, Pueblo Indians. They are neither as prosperous nor as skilful as their forefathers were. Changes in the climate have reduced the rivers, dried the canals, and parched the country until all the fertile fields have disappeared, and the people have a hard time to make a living. They have suffered other losses, too, from the raids of wild Apaches and other Indians living to the north and west of them.

Pottery is still made in the old pueblos, but not with the skill of olden times. The Spaniards, who found the Pueblos, called them a wonderful people and admired their work and their prowess in war; but the Spaniards taught them new customs which did much to change their lives. Moreover, here and everywhere, when the Spaniard saw anything he wanted, he took it, from the son of a chief to wait upon him, to a curiously moulded dish or a bright-colored blanket. The Pueblos of to-day are descendants of a race who were taught something of the Roman Catholic religion and something of the Spanish language and of many Spanish customs, all of which they have mingled with their inheritance from earlier times.

THE DUCKING OF THE CLOWNS.

One of the most amusing of the Pueblo customs is what they call "ducking the clowns." If you were at the Zuñi pueblo in the month of July,

DU-ME-CHIM-CHEE, OR, THE DUCKING OF THE CLOWNS.

you might see this strange ceremony. All the men and women of the pueblos are out of doors, on the terraces, and on the ground. Presently, ten men, who live in the house, come out. They are dressed in coarse, blue cloth, and wear horrible masks of mud. First, they form a line, as you see in the picture. Each one bends over and places his hands on the hips of the man before him. In a moment they start to run around the outside or back-walls of the pueblo, singing "Du-me-chim-chee, Du-me-chim-chee," over and over again, while the crowd shout and laugh. The women on the walls above "duck" them with jars of water, some of it clean, some dirty. One girl after another has her jar full and waiting for them to come by her terrace. It is an old ceremony, called "ducking the clowns," and everyone, young and old, delights in it, the "clowns" as much as the others. Troops of children usually follow the "clowns," and if they get some of the water, the greater is the fun.

This frolic is part of a long religious ceremony. The next day a priest leads a party to the Sacred Lake to carry offerings to the rain gods, and to pray for rains upon their dry land in summer.

THE ANNUAL POTTERY BAKING.

While the priest and his attendants are praying for rain at the Sacred Lake, the women of the pueblo bake or "fire" all the decorated pots and bowls and clay animals that have been made in the past weeks. I have seen a picture of a Pueblo woman and her daughter at this work. Their pottery is piled in heaps of dirt, about which the fires are lighted. They hold a blanket to protect the fire from the wind. You see a picture of one of their vases in the corner of the large picture of the Pueblo house.

TIHUS.

The little girls in the pueblos have dolls or tihus to play with. They are made to represent gods. Here is the picture of one—curious-looking, isn't it? These dolls, made and dressed by the mothers, are used in religious ceremonies, and to teach the children of the pueblos many ideas about their gods. After that the children have them to play with.

THE PARENT RACE.

Some ethnologists believe that all these early people of America—the Pueblos, the Cliff-dwellers, the Mound-builders, and the Midden-men came from one race, which lived in Central America, and were the builders of the wonderful structures which are found there to-day. If you put your pencil on your maps at Central America, and draw a line to the Pueblo States of New Mexico, Arizona, Utah and Colorado; then go back and draw another line from Central America to the Ohio Valley; and still other lines to the Atlantic and the

CALAKO MANA; OR, THE CORN MAIDEN.

Pacific coasts, you will see that one race may have sent out emigrants in all these directions. They may have gone at various times, and for various reasons. They went to different places, and they may have mingled with more barbaric races than their own. War, perhaps, was made on them as intruders. All of these conditions had much to do with changing their habits and customs, until after a few generations they were like a different people. Probably they forgot their parent race, as their descendants have forgotten them. Men interested in such things might never have thought of the connection if they had not found the remains, which are carefully kept now in our museums. When we compare the vases and tools made by the Pueblos with those made by the Cliff-dwellers and Mound-builders of the United States, and all with the finer things made by the ancient people of Central America, we see that the peoples may have been related to each other in some way, and probably came from the same race; but if they did, they grew far apart before the time when they made the things we have seen.

CHAPTER IV.

THE INDIANS.

The first real history we have of our country is in the reports made by voyagers from Europe near the beginning of the sixteenth century. Those voyagers found a race here, whom they called Indians, because they thought the country was a part of India. The natives were also called salvages, or savages, because they did not have the customs, called civilization, of Europe and the Orient. Because they did not know the Christian religion, they were called heathen. We know that some of the Indians were descendants of the Pueblos. Many people think that others were from the Midden-men and Cave-dwellers, the Mound-builders and Cliff-dwellers. Most of the Indians of to-day have forgotten the customs and arts of their forefathers, whom the Europeans first saw.

We know but little of what they were then, however; for the Europeans brought many things to the Indians that changed their customs, especially their industries, before any record was made of them. Up to that time the natives made everything for themselves; but as soon as they saw the bright-colored clothing, the glass beads, tin cups, and the showy trinkets of the Europeans, they willingly gave any quantity of their own things for them.

NATIVE MANUFACTURES.

The Europeans carried these products home, to show their kings and countrymen what manner of people they had found in the New World. They took fabrics of yucca fibre, of dog-bane, of bark, and of goat-hair. They took clay vases and jars, shell-work, and articles made of stone, of bone, and of many other things.

The natives ceased to make most of them as soon as they found that the strangers would bring their bright things over in large quantities and barter them for the skins of animals, which the Indians trapped and shot with the strangers' guns far more easily than with their own bows and arrows. With the new beads and coarse, red flannel they made new things to please the Europeans, as the articles from across the seas pleased themselves. So it was not very long before the life of the natives which they had lived by themselves for hundreds of years, perhaps, was entirely changed. Few voyagers learned enough about it to give us the true picture of it. The most that we know of our red men is of the red men under European influences.

HOW THE INDIANS LOOKED.

The natives who lived here when the first Europeans came dressed far differently from any you may see now; but in face and figure there has been little change. Almost all of them had dark skins, straight, black hair, low and receding foreheads, black eyes, high cheek-bones, flat noses, white teeth under big lips, and no beards. Their figures were tall and straight, often plump, yet almost never fat. Europeans spoke of the children and young men and women as "comely," and of the old men and women as "uglie." Their hair was worn in different ways. In the South one side of the head was shaved clean, and from the other the hair hung in a long braid or tied bunch. Some tribes wore all the hair cut short, except enough to make one long "pig-tail" from the middle of the head. Others left a single strip through the middle of the head, which stuck up like a cock's comb.

DRESS.

Feathers have always been used as ornaments, sometimes in garments, sometimes in head-dresses, and sometimes as single feathers, cut and painted to show various degrees of honors won in war.

The Indians, especially in the warm, Southern countries, wore little clothing, sometimes no more than a kind of short skirt, which did not reach to their knees. About their necks the Indians hung strings of beads, or the polished teeth of animals, strings of birds' claws, squirrels' heads, and many such ornaments. In colder parts of the country deer and bears' skins were worn in winter, with the fur left on the pelt. Large, warm garments were sometimes made of many small skins sewed together. They were from such animals as the otter, beaver and raccoon. For summer wear lighter skins were chosen. Sometimes the fur was scraped off for summer garments. For hunting in thickets, the men had a sort of leather breeches. They had leggings or socks of skins, too, and low shoes, called moccasins.

The customs in dress were changed by Europeans before almost any others. This was partly because the white men thought their own way of dressing was the only right and proper way, but more, perhaps, because they wanted the skins to sell to the merchants at home.

A Dutch trader said that the natives were eager to barter their fine furs for common red flannel, which they wrapped loosely about them, and glanced down upon with a grin of satisfaction. From that time to this, the dress of the Indians has been a funny mixture of Indian and European fashions and materials.

In the pictures of Indians in this book you can see what things you think they made themselves, and what were probably made by Europeans.

QUEEN OHOLASC.

William Strachey, an Englishman, writing about Virginia in 1618, described the dress of Queen Oholase, Powhatan's wife. You may get two things from what he says. One is a picture of the queen and her wardrobe. The other is the fun of trying to tell his quaint story in your own language. Strachey says: "I was once early at her house, yt being sommertime, when she was layed without dores, under the shadowe of a broad leaved tree, upon a pallett of osiers, spred over with four or five fyne grey matts, herself covered with a faire white drest deere skynne or two, and when she rose, she had a mayd who fetcht her a frontall [a forehead ornament] of white currall and pendants of great but imperfect conloured and worse drilled pearles, which she put into her eares, and a chayne with long lyncks of copper which

TROTTING WOLF AND SQUAW.

they call Tapoantaminais, and which came twice or thrice about her necke and they accompt a jolly ornament, and sure thus attired with some variety of feathers and flowers stuck in their haires, they seem as debonaire, quaynt, and well pleased as a daughter of the house of Austria behune [decked] with all her jewels; likewise her mayd fetcht her a mantill made of blue feathers so artificially and thick sewed togither, that it seemed like a deepe purple satten, and is very smooth and sleeke; and after she brought her water for her hands, and then a branch or twoo of fresh greene ashen leaves as for a towell to dry them."

PAINTING AND TATTOOING.

The Indians did not keep their skin sleek and smooth to show the swarthy hue. They painted themselves in many colors. To make these decorations the more lasting, the patterns were sometimes pricked deeply into the skin with thorns and the thorn holes filled with paint, much like the tattooing still done in the South Pacific Islands and other places. One of the old voyagers said, "Many forms of paintings they use; but he is the most gallant who is the most monstrous and ugly to behold."

The Indians' faces and hands, and often nearly

the whole of their bodies, were tattooed in this way or painted for special occasions.

KINSHIP AND TOTEMS.

Indian children had no opportunity to be lonely. They lived near their grandparents, uncles and aunts. They had dozens of cousins to play with. In fact, their "families" were clans. A village was usually made up of a group of families related to each other and bound together to help one another, to live and to die for one another, if necessary. Each such clan had an emblem, called a "totem," somewhat as the old clans in Europe had their colors and their coats-of-arms. The totem was a bird, a turtle, a fish, or some other familiar thing. Images were made of it in wood or stone. Representations of it were carved on shells, worn about the neck, or worn in belts or blankets; and often a rude picture of it was tattooed on the men's bodies. In one way or another the totem was worn as a badge by members of the clan. It was also used as a signature in declarations of war, in treaties, in boundary agreements and in other

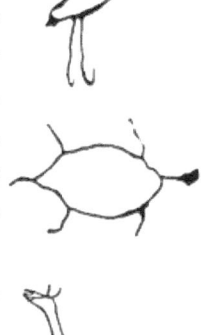

TOTEMS OF NEW ENGLAND INDIANS.

matters of business with other clans, and with the white men after the colonists came.

VILLAGES.

One of these large clans made a village by itself, and the village was a group of huts or wigwams. They did not always live in the same place the year round. In summer, they were usually on the bank of a river, or the shore of a bay where there was good fishing. Toward winter, when the hunting season came on, the whole village removed to the edge of a forest.

SKIN COVERED WIGWAM

The huts or wigwams were made in many ways. Some were of young trees set in the ground in a circle for a small hut, in two long rows for a large one. They were bent over at the top and fastened together, all covered with bark. Sometimes the young trees or poles were driven in the ground at such an angle that they slanted toward the top and crossed at the ends. A hole was left for smoke, and the rest of the frame-work was closely covered with bark on the outside, and with skins

THE TOWN OF POMEIOOC.

on the inside. The long wigwams were usually so placed that the doors in each end looked toward the north and the south. According to the way of the wind, one or the other was nearly always open, to make the proper draft for the fire. We might not call it a proper draft, but the Indians were satisfied if it sent enough smoke through the hole in the top of the hut, to make the fire burn. The wigwam door was like a rude gate, covered by a piece of bark or skin. These doors were fastened with wooden pins when they were fastened at all.

ABBINOS.

There was nothing of what we call furniture in the wigwams, not even beds. Everyone sat and slept on skins and on mats woven from rushes by the women. These were thrown upon the ground, but all the men and women had their own mats and skins and their own places for them and for their own belongings, which they kept behind their mats. These spaces were called abbinos. They were on the bare earth, for the wigwams had no other floors. The Indian mother always assigned the abbinos to each of the family when they settled in a new place, and to the visitor when they had company. Every new baby was taught to toddle to its mother's mat, and no one dared to take another's place or to meddle with the things kept there.

A visitor among the Indians in New Netherland, said: "It is their custom to sleep only on the bare ground, and to have only a stone or bit of wood under their heads."

MOVING.

The people who lived in these simple dwellings found moving an easy matter. When the men decided to go from the seashore to the mountains, the women made a few compact bundles of the skins, the cooking utensils, and the other durable things they used, hoisted them on their backs and followed their men-folks to their new building lots. When they had horses, the horses carried the baggage on trailing poles.

In the new home fresh poles were cut and the families were soon settled in new huts, which for a short time were rather clean.

POWHATAN'S STOREHOUSE.

In Isenacommacah, which was the Indian name for Virginia, the great chief, Powhatan, had a big storehouse, quite different from the wigwams. William Strachey said that it stood in a thicket of wood, that it was the chief's storehouse for his treasures, such as skins, copper, pearls and beads. "which he storeth upp against the time of his death and buryall." There also he kept his store of red paint for ointment, and his bows and arrows. "This howse is fifty or sixty yards in length, frequented only by priests. At four corners of the howse stand four images as careful sentinells to defend and protect the howse; one is like a dragon, another like a bear, the third like a leopard, and the fourth a giant-like man." All were as ugly to look upon as the workmanship of the Indians could make them.

CHAPTER V.

INDIAN CHILDREN.

When an Indian baby was born, its father and mother did not show their tenderness for it as yours do. The mother did not wrap the little thing in soft, white flannel, or nestle it in her arms, and keep the whole family quiet while it slept. She wrapped the hardy a-bin-o-jee, as it was called, in a piece of coarse blanket, or some animal's skin, and strapped it upon a board, which she carried on her back, or hung on a tree while she was at work. Yet she seems to have taken much pride in ornamenting this rough cradle, which is called tikkinagon. Sometimes she trimmed it with beads, bright shells, or cloth dyed in gay colors; some of these bright objects were where the baby could see them, or play with them.

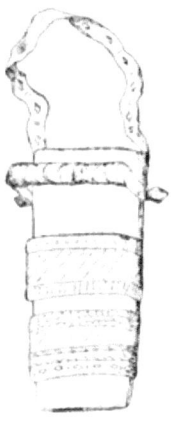
Indian Cradle Board.

Miss Alice Fletcher, a lady who has been among

the Indians for a long time, says that the a-bin-o-jee now-a-days is taken out of its tikkinagon every day, to receive its bath, and to frolic with its mother, or small brothers and sisters, before it is strapped up again out of everyone's way. In time it learned to walk. Then the mother often carried it "pig-back" for a while, holding it by one hand and one foot. You may think that neither of these ways of being carried was comfortable for the little one; but they were the best its mother could do, for she worked hard all the time. The brothers and sisters had to work, too. The fathers were off hunting and fishing, or at their wars. So the babies grew up without much attention from any one.

HAPPY CHILDREN.

The little Indians were happy children, Mr. Schoolcraft said, when writing about them—and Mr. Schoolcraft was a man who lived among the Indians to learn their ways. It has been said that he knew more about them than any other white man ever knew. He wrote that they had many pleasures, and that the fathers and mothers cheerfully went hungry when food was scarce to give it to the little ones.

Cruel and harsh the Indian was to his enemies, but to his friends and his family he was as kind as he knew how to be. The children had toys, made by their hard-working mothers. Their fathers took great care to teach them the things Indians thought important to know. Their larger broth-

FOLLOW MY LEADER.

From Indian Songs collected by Miss Alice G. Fletcher. By permission of Peabody Museum.

ers and sisters taught them games and songs, such as "Follow my Leader," in which the little ones trot along in time to a song.

A FATHER'S LOVE FOR HIS SON.

Mr. Schoolcraft tells this story of Bi-ans-wah: In the war between the Chippewas and the Foxes, the Foxes captured the son of a celebrated and aged chief of the Chippewas, named Bi-ans-wah, while the father was absent from his wigwam.

On reaching home, the old man heard the heart-rending news, and, knowing what the fate of his son would be, he followed on the trail of the enemy alone. He reached the Fox villages just as they were kindling the fire to roast the son alive. He stepped boldly into the arena and offered to take his son's place:

"My son," said he, "has seen but a few winters; his feet have never trod the war-path; but the hairs of my head are white; I have hung many scalps over the graves of my relatives, which I have taken from the heads of your warriors; kindle the fire about me, and send my son home to my lodge." The offer was accepted, and the old man, without a groan, was burnt at the stake.

WHEN AN INDIAN CHILD DIED.

The burial of a child was much simpler than that of the warrior; but the grief of his father and mother was very deep. The warrior had won his honors on the war-path; the baby would never grow up to have his chance to win them. The parents often comforted themselves by adopting a boy, and if no Indian father and mother would give up their son, the sad father and mother would steal one from the white people on the frontier, not thinking of the sorrow they caused, but filled with the one idea that they must have a boy, for all the hopes of the Indian family were centred in their boys.

THE SMALL BOYS.

The father never took care of the baby; but if it were a boy, he watched eagerly for the time when it could use its first tiny bow and arrow. As soon as the Indian boy could toddle about, he was taught to handle his little bow, and to shoot birds and squirrels. His first game, however small, was cooked for a dinner, to which were invited all the little man's great relatives—even the chiefs.

The Indian small boy learned to set traps very early, too. Sometimes, of course, they were not very well set, but the fathers looked after them, and often secretly put animals in, to encourage the little fellows to try again.

Soon the toy bow and arrows were laid aside for stronger ones; but there were many things to learn besides merely to shoot. The boy must know what birds he should find in May, and what ones in October. He was taught the birds' colors, how one differed from another in delicate shades of breast and wing, in beak and foot. He learned their calls, and the meaning of them, and he watched them until he knew all their habits.

An Indian Boy.

About animals, he learned in the same way where rabbits and hares burrowed; in what underbrush it was easiest to catch them; and hundreds of things that all American boys want to know to this day.

By the time the leaves had returned twelve seasons, which was the way Indians reckoned years, the boy usually knew how to make and to use his large bow and arrow, how to make canoes and quintans, and many other things. He knew how to fish and to hunt for large game. Probably he had begun to go alone on dangerous undertakings, and his father had begun to teach him some of the many things a warrior must know.

HOW QUINTANS WERE MADE.

Perhaps the boys enjoyed boat-making better than anything else except hunting. From this picture you can describe their boat-making for yourselves. You can see just how the trees were burned down near the roots, the branches and the tops burned off, leaving logs of the right length for boats. The logs were then burned out on one side and the charred wood scraped out with shells. Then the rude-shaped boats called quintans were considered ready for use. Besides this kind of a boat, the Indians have probably

MAKING A BOAT.

always made canoes of light frames covered with bark.

BOWS AND ARROWS.

The work of making bows and arrows must have taken considerable time. Think of the hundreds of arrow-shafts each Indian must have whittled and the many arrow-heads he must have chipped out of flint and other stone. Some of these were poisoned by dipping them into a curious mixture, made, so one Englishman said, of fair red apples, which were poisonous, and of venemous bats and vipers.

HUNTING AND FISHING

were important. The boys learned both as they grew up, because the life of all depended on them. There were no stores then, of course, and no markets. Each father was his own hunter and fisherman, butcher and fishman. The boys began very young to fish. In summer they fished from the shore or from the canoe. In winter, they fished in curious ways; sometimes through holes in the ice with hook and line; sometimes with a long spear. This spear was shaped like a fish on the pointed end. The Indian made a hole in the ice, sat down beside it, pulled a blanket over himself, head and all, in order to make the water dark beneath him, so that the fish would come up to the make-believe fish, suspecting nothing. Then the Indian's spear would go right through him. These skilful hunters and fishermen had many tricks to catch their game easily or in quantity when they needed much of it. Sometimes when they found a herd of deer in woods near the shore, they drove the whole herd upon some narrow point of land running far into the water, and cut off all escape by building a row of fires across the neck to the mainland. So they kept the herd in a preserve until all the deer that were wanted had been shot.

WHAT DID THE INDIANS EAT?

You know that they ate game and fish of all kinds, and both fresh and dried. They knew all the edible fruits, roots, nuts and other products of forest and plains. You will find that the first Europeans who visited them were interested in their maize, or corn and the cakes they made with it. All the Indians we have any records of have used potatoes in many ways. The wild potatoes now have curious little roots, no larger than good-

Kaus Root is pounded and is mixed in the water and baked on the fire, each loaf resting on a stick. Nez Percés Indians, Idaho.

BROILING FISH

sized peanuts. Out of another root the Indians have long made a sort of flat, oblong cake, called Kaus Bread. The women dry the roots, grind them, mix them with water, and then flatten them into cakes. The dough must be tough, for a cake is baked before the fire, while hanging by two sticks run through it, near the centre. You may see the holes in the picture. Some people say that the red men eat the roots of water-lilies. How do you suppose they taste?

For drink the natives generally used clear water. They made a great variety of beverages with the berries, leaves and roots they knew. The drinks brought by Europeans pleased them better than their own. Although rum and whiskey crazed the savages and did more than anything else to ruin them, yet they would barter anything they had for the white man's "fire water," as they called it.

GOOD TIMES.

The boys and girls who play Indian seem to think the Indians did nothing but scalp their enemies and steal white people's children. Perhaps you know that they did many other things, but think it is more fun to play warrior than anything else. Or perhaps you do not know much about the other interesting things they did. They had many sports and games for the children and the grown-up Indians. There was a game of ball on the grass. Another, much like hockey, was played with sticks on the ice. Lacrosse, the favorite sport in Canada, is an Indian game.

MAPLE SUGAR.

The making of maple sugar, which is the best fun of the year in some parts of New England, is an old Indian custom. They held their seensibankwit, or sugar-making carnival every year, all joining in the fun. The children carried the sap in pails of bark from the trees to the place where it was boiled in great kettles brought over by the Europeans. Perhaps before the strangers came they had soapstone vats or kettles. At any rate, no one now knows of a time when the Indians did not make delicious maple sugar, and when they did not have their "sugaring off" every spring.

PLUM-STONES.

Another game was called plum-stones, because it was played with the stones of wild plums. Some of them were in their natural state when dried. Others were carved and painted with figures of birds and animals. Plain stones and decorated stones were put together in a low, round bowl, shaken, much as you shake dice in a box for parchesi, and thrown on a smooth skin spread upon the ground. The counts in the game were reckoned by the figured stones that fell on the skin right side up.

There is a special song which the winner sings.

WAR AND WARRIORS.

The joy of an Indian father was to see his son a warrior. For that, he taught the boy to be skilful and brave, and from the time he gave the toddler his first little bow and arrow, the Indian's rule for his sons was, " never to blame timidity, but to praise bravery."

To take part in a war-dance was the highest ambition of every Indian boy; for when he entered the circle of warriors, and joined in this dance to the music of gourds and rattles, he was enlisted for war. To the Indian, the only way to honor and distinction was the war-path.

Our American boys may become great men—governors of the states, or presidents of the United States, and yet know nothing of war. They may be inventors, such as Edison, great business men, professors in colleges, judges in high courts; they may win great honors in many ways, without knowing how to use a gun; but the only honors for an Indian came as rewards for success in war. In that way he could win the admiration and respect of his tribe and others. In that way he could rise to the head of his people, to be their counsellor, their sachem, or their chief.

Before the Indian lad could hope to take his one path to glory, he had many things to learn. He made, as well as used, his bows and arrows. Besides his hunting, he practiced at a mark until he could hit a very small object at a very great distance. He learned how warriors took the scalps of their enemies, and how they were cured and fastened to shields and belts.

THE WAR-DANCES.

Hours the Indian lad spent with his brothers and cousins practicing the dances which the warriors danced with great skill. When he was about sixteen years of age, he was considered old enough to go to war, and was allowed to respond to a call for warriors among his clan. That was when some leader or war-captain, with a club in his hand and red paint on his face, gathered the men and youth about him to tell them that he wished to raise a party to attack some enemy, and would lead all who offered to go. This he told partly in song.

partly in short-spoken sentences with piercing yells every few minutes, flourishing his war-club all the time, and singing

AN INDIAN WAR-SONG.

Hear my voice, ye warlike birds!
I prepare a feast for you to fatten on;
I see you cross the enemy's lines;
Like you I shall go.

I wish the swiftness of your wings;
I wish the vengeance of your claws;
I muster my friends;
I follow your flight.

Ho, ye young men, that are warriors,
Look with wrath on the battle-field.

As he sang and shouted, the warriors gathered about him to show their willingness to join his expedition. This was the chance for the Indian lad, and when he stepped to the warriors' circle and joined the war-dance, he stepped from boyhood into manhood.

ON THE WAR-PATH.

The dance finished, the lad provided himself with weapons and food, and went off on the war-path. Here his work was cruel, for he not only killed his enemies but also cut off the scalp of each one of them, flourished it by its long hair, over his head, and hung it by his side, where he often looked at it with pleasure. Afterward each scalp was stretched on a frame to dry and carried about in later war-dances and wars. For his success, the Indian was allowed to wear feathers in his head, differing in kind and number according to his triumphs. To wear an eagle's feather was considered the greatest honor. No one could wear such a badge unless it was publicly awarded.

GIRLS AND WOMEN.

While the Indian men were on the war-path, or hunting and fishing, the women did many kinds of work which we expect men to do. The girls began very young to help their mothers. They cooked and sewed and kept their wigwams in order. This was not what we would call housekeeping. They never swept; they had nothing like our furniture. The floor, upon which the family sat, slept and ate, was very dirty, and swarmed with insects; but no one minded that. The women cut and handed the wood for the fires, which in summer were outside the wigwams, while in winter they were inside, for both warmth and cooking.

Both boys and girls helped their mothers in planting the corn and tobacco, considering it a great frolic.

AFTER THE GAME WAS SHOT.

Some of the hardest work the women did was to fetch home the large game. After the hunter had shot his deer or bear, he sometimes turned his back on it, broke a branch from some tree near by, to make a trail of its leaves, and strode off to his wigwam. On reaching home, he gave a leaf of his trail to his wife or squaw. She and some other women and girls of the family followed the leaf-trail till they found the game, which they carried home. They skinned it, took out the sinews for their sewing and other purposes, cut up the meat and cooked it. The skin they stretched on a rough frame to dry. Then they cured it, and made it up into shirts or breeches, perhaps, and the smaller pieces into moccasins.

EMBROIDERY AND POTTERY-MAKING.

The girls began when young to embroider with brightly-polished shells, pebbles, and bits of mica, until real beads were brought them by the traders from Europe. Can you imagine how delighted they were with the bright-colored glass beads, and with bright-red flannel?

The making of dishes for cooking, and of vases or jars for carrying water, was women's work, too. Often these toiling mothers and big sisters made earthen ducks, with seeds or pebbles inside, for the babies to play with, and sometimes they made queer, animal-shaped dishes for the older children, somewhat like the bear-jug and duck-dish found in the grave of the mound-builder's child. Probably the children soon learned to make these dishes by watching their mothers and trying by themselves. If you have clay-modeling at school, you can try to make some of these duck-dishes and bear-jugs for yourselves.

INDIAN BURIALS.

When the Indian father saw his son become an honored warrior, he was ready to leave this world and go, as he said, to the "happy hunting ground." He felt that the most important work of his life was accomplished.

After he died, his body was dressed in new skins of animals or a blanket; new moccasins were put on his feet; and the feathers which he

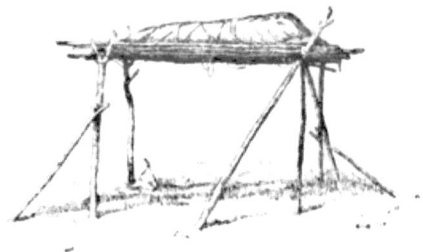
SCAFFOLD BURIAL.

had won the right in war to wear were placed on his head. Then the body was wrapped in cloth or bark. In some parts of the country the Indians were buried in graves, but not deeply, and were protected by branches and stones. Sometimes the body was put into a canoe with another canoe fitted closely over it. At other times the corpse was laid upon a platform, raised high enough from the ground to be out of the reach of dogs or wild animals. There was need to protect the dead body from animals, but not from other Indians, for they would not disturb the dead of even their enemies. The warrior's arms were laid beside him, and after they began to have horses, his war-steed, too, was killed and left at the grave, so that the warrior might have him in the next life. Food was left near the grave, and sometimes a bundle of sticks, showing how many ponies he had given away. These, with other odd decorations, told the passer-by what honors the Indian warrior had in life.

CHAPTER VI.

PIONEERS FROM EUROPE.

You know how often little children wonder if there are people in the moon. Perhaps you have longed to go to it yourselves to find who lived there. Perhaps there is some lonely road which runs over a hill or is lost in a wood, where you have never been allowed to go, but which you have wished to see and about which you have had all sorts of fancies. Perhaps you have imagined all kinds of animals which might tear you in pieces, and men who might treat you cruelly. Still you have dreamed of lovely things which might be there and, in spite of fear, have wished to go in search of them. Can each one of you remember some such ideas and feelings about strange places?

OLD IDEAS ABOUT THE EARTH.

The people in Europe in the fifteenth century used to have these same strange fancies about the far-off land to the west across the Atlantic Ocean. There had been a time when people did not imagine that there was any other land besides their own.

The earth they thought to be a flat surface, something the shape of a large shield. Some believed there was one large ocean surrounding the land they knew. Others thought there was an edge or rim of land outside the surrounding waters, which was joined on all sides by the sky fitting over it like a big dome. Some men said that the earth was of a much more beautiful, perfect shape; it was not a plane, but a sphere. Then they began to think that if it were round a man could travel around it as a fly can walk around an apple. For centuries these ideas were merely talked about. Then for several centuries more they were nearly forgotten. They were written on rolls of parchment, which were the books of those days; but those books were hidden away and known only to a few great scholars.

TRAVEL TO THE HOLY LAND.

A custom had grown up among the Christians of Europe of making pilgrimages to Jerusalem. Men and women wanted to visit the sacred spots where Christ had lived and died. They were often hindered and harmed by the Turks and Saracens who lived in and about the Holy Land. These were heathen, whom the Christians of Europe wished to conquer and convert. For this, large

ORIENTAL SCENE.

military expeditions, called crusades, were undertaken, as early as 1100, by the great warriors and humble peasants of all parts of Europe. Thousands went armed to the Holy Land to snatch the sacred places from the heathen Turks and Saracens.

While there, the Europeans became used to the Oriental luxuries which these people had gotten from the people living still further to the east.

ORIENTAL LUXURIES.

These Orientals had beautiful silks, linens, jewels, ivories, fine spices, delicious dried fruits, and many other luxuries that Europeans delighted in. Indeed, the people of the West liked these things so much that merchants soon began to send for them. They sent out parties of traders in large caravans, with camels and horses. They soon opened regular routes of travel for their trade from India and from China. In the early part of the fifteenth century these trade routes were closed by the Turks, who took possession of the country through which the caravans passed, and refused to allow the Europeans to enter it.

THE WESTERN PASSAGE.

Then the most learned and the most enterprising men of Europe tried to think of some other way to get the silks and spices from the Orient to Europe. Every one talked of a new route to the East. Geographers and navigators began to examine the old books and maps, and to think that if the world was round, perhaps they could find India or Cathay by sailing westward out of the Mediterranean Sea, and across the western or Atlantic Ocean. Merchant sailors from Venice, in Italy, had passed out of the Mediterranean, through the narrow straits of Gibraltar, and, after passing beyond the shores of Portugal and France, had found their way to the ports of England.

Portuguese sailors, inspired by their king, Henry the Navigator, had crept gradually down along the shores of Africa, discovered the coast and the islands, and returned in safety.

Most people, however, believed the stories that had been handed down for centuries, about horrible monsters that lived in the western waters. Mothers and wives were filled with terror when their sons and husbands talked of sailing out upon this unknown ocean, which was called the Sea of Darkness. The men, too, were superstitious. They believed that all sorts of impossible things might happen. Yet enough sailors to man a fleet could generally be found for almost any undertaking. Love of adventure was strong in the hearts of the

SEA OF DARKNESS.

descendants of the Teuton people, who once lived in the forests of Germany, fighting wild beasts and delighting in stories of how their wonderful ancestors killed dragons and all sorts of monsters that guarded hoards of gold in dark and enchanted caves. It was the hope of finding treasure as much as love of adventure that induced the sailors of the fifteenth century to ship on voyages of discovery across the Sea of Darkness.

CHRISTOPHER COLUMBUS, THE WORLD'S SEA HERO.
1492 1506.

The greatest men of that age were the leaders of these voyages, the men who could take the responsibility of the ship's course in strange waters, who could command the crew, whose hearts were above fear and despair when even their bravest men lost hope, begged to go back, and finally threatened the lives of their commanders if the fleets were not turned homeward. Such men of ability and courage were found in every nation of Europe during the sixteenth and seventeenth centuries; but he who came first of all was the great admiral, Christopher Columbus.

The world knows little of his life. We do not know how he looked. You often see pictures and statues of him, but they show merely what his face and figure were supposed to be by painters and sculptors of later times. So you may all picture him for yourselves, while you read of what he did.

He was born, a poor boy, at Genoa, in Italy, at about 1435. His father, who was probably a wool-comber, gave his boy " the ordinary schooling of his time and a touch of university life." At fourteen he became a sailor. This was an exciting life for the lad, and the quieter work of selling books at Genoa some time later must have made him restless for the sea again. Yet this may have given him an opportunity to study old maps and read books written by old geographers. He knew their theories of the size and shape of the earth. He made himself master, also, of the newest theories and arts of navigation in his own times. Perhaps he made maps and charts with his older brother. After that he went to Portugal, and from there he made several short voyages; but we shall not follow them.

HIS GREAT AIM.

We shall follow Columbus only in the one great aim of his life. This was to cross the western seas and reach the Orient. He asked many great people to help him do it, and was laughed at in answer; but, at last, Queen Isabella and King Ferdinand of Spain took an interest in him.

They borrowed money to fit out a fleet, and gave him royal authority, as their great admiral, to sail westward and discover new lands for Spain. The joy of Columbus was so great that he promised to spend his share in the profits of his discoveries in another crusade to secure the holy places in Jerusalem. His little son, Diego, was made a page in the king's household, and then Columbus went to the seaport, Palos where the king had ordered three vessels to be prepared for him.

The people of Palos did not receive Columbus kindly. They did not like his undertaking to cross the broad Atlantic Ocean. He had a hard time to persuade sailors to go out with him. They were sure that they would be eaten by monsters or sail off the edge of the world. With the help of two friends named Pinzon, the admiral made up his small fleet of three vessels, fitted them out with food and all necessary provisions, and at last found men enough for their crews. They set sail August 3, 1492. Columbus was in command of the fleet and of the largest vessel, the *Santa Maria*. The Pinzon brothers were in charge of the two other vessels, the *Nina* and the *Pinta*, which were smaller, and called caravels. All of the captains believed that if they came to land across the Atlantic it would be on some unknown eastern shore of Asia, the land of spices.

Columbus first went down to the Canary Islands off the west coast of Africa. They were known to him. He believed that they were about opposite India. So he took his westward course from them. When the fleet left the Canaries it was indeed on an unknown sea. Day and night it sailed, and it passed out of sight of land, a fact which frightened the sailors as much as the big waves did. Everyone knows that the waves of the Atlantic dip and rise until they sometimes seem like mountains in height. The sailors soon began to grumble. As day after day passed with no sign of land, the men lost all hope. They threatened mutiny. Then they utterly refused to do their work unless the admiral would turn back. In all these difficulties Columbus was steadfast in his purpose. He was determined that nothing should turn him from it. He told the men so. He was commander by order of the king and queen, and he would be obeyed. He wished to keep straight on. If he had done so, he would have found the northern continent, probably near the mouth of what we call Delaware Bay.

THE NEW LAND.

On the Pinzon brothers' advice, the Admiral altered the course to a southerly direction, and by that means, in the early morning of the 12th of

October, a mariner on the *Pinta* saw a small island of the Bahama group. The natives called it Guanahani, Columbus said; he named it San Salvador, which is Spanish for Holy Savior. From there the discoverers went to the much larger island which Columbus called Juana, and we know as Cuba; then to Hayti, which was named Hispaniola or Little Spain. There they anchored. One of the fleet was wrecked on the coast of this island, and Columbus used her timbers to build a fort, which he called La Navidad.

On his way back to Spain, Columbus wrote a letter to Santangel, a man who had loaned to Ferdinand and Isabella much of the money they spent in fitting out the fleet. The letter began:

"Sir—As I know you will be rejoiced at the glorious success that our Lord has given me in my voyage, I write this to tell you how, in thirty-three days, I sailed to the Indies.

"It has many ports along the sea-coast, and many fine, large, flowing rivers. The land there is elevated, with many mountains and peaks. They are most beautiful, of a thousand varied forms, accessible, and full of trees of endless varieties, so high that they seem to touch the sky, and I have been told that they never lose their foliage. . . . The nightingale, and other small birds of a thousand

A SCENE IN THE NEW WORLD.

kinds, were singing in the month of November, when I was there. . . . There are wonderful pine trees, and very extensive ranges of meadow land. There is honey, and a great variety of fruits. Inland there are numerous mines of metals, and innumerable people.

"There are many spices and vast mines of gold . . . in this island. . . . I have found no monsters, as some expected; but, on the contrary, they are people of very handsome appearance."   "Hispaniola is a marvel."

THE NEWS IN SPAIN.

The discovery was received in Spain as the most wonderful news that ever was heard. Columbus was then the Great Admiral to every one, and the hero of the world. Ferdinand and Isabella received him at court, as you see in the picture. They received him with high honors, seated upon their thrones, wearing their crowns, dressed in their royal robes of state, with their courtiers in attendance—all to hear the story of his voyage, and his discoveries, and to see what he had brought back with him. All marveled most at the natives he had coaxed or tricked to come aboard his ship. Such people had never been seen nor heard of before. Since they came from India they were called Indians, though they were unlike the peo-

ple of East India, except that both were dark-skinned and heathen. The western Indians were savages, with straight, black hair and uncouth manners; they wore odd-looking garments, and were decorated with feathers and paint.

We can easily imagine how the king and queen and the people of Spain talked about these wonders and the new land. Think of the women of Palos, who had been opposed to the voyage. How much they had to "take back," as they talked about it at their marketing, and in their homes. Many visits were made, for the purpose, no doubt, of discussing the wonderful reports. All the sailors who had gone on the voyage returned heroes, even if they had done their utmost to ruin the expedition, and had threatened to kill the admiral unless he turned back long before the new land was found.

Not many years before this the art of printing had been discovered. The story of Columbus's voyage was printed and sent out over Europe, a double wonder, for people were as eager to see a piece of print as they were to learn of the West Indies.

As the news spread throughout Europe, all the great navigators wanted to join Columbus, or to follow his example in ventures of their own. The sailors of every port had lost all fear of the Sea of Darkness. "Now," he wrote, "there is not a man, down to the very tailors, who does not beg to be allowed to become a discoverer."

THE SECOND VOYAGE.

It was easy to man and fit out a second expedition, although it was a fleet of seventeen vessels. Ferdinand and Isabella decided to plant a colony in Little Spain, and twelve hundred people sailed with the great admiral in September, 1494.

When Columbus reached Hispaniola he found his fort, La Navidad, in ruins; but he set his men to work at once to build a town, which he called Isabella. Other men gathered products of the islands, which were sent back, with some natives, in the colonists' ships. Still others began to hunt for gold. Columbus had made everyone believe as he did, that large quantities of gold would be found with little trouble. Too eager to await the results of their own labor, the colonists set the natives at work digging in what they called their mines. They were hard task-masters, and as the digging went on and no gold was found, they grew harsher and more cruel to the Indians.

ANGER OF THE NATIVES.

The Indians, for their part, resented this treatment from the strangers. The savages had given

RUINS OF LA NAVIDAD.

the white men a kindly welcome. It was their custom to do all in their power for their guests; but to give generously in hospitality was one thing, and to have their guests make slaves of them was quite another. They were not used to such hard work as this. They showed that they did not wish to do it. When the Spaniards drove them to it, they began to dislike their visitors. Soon they began to show their dislike, and to take measures to protect themselves.

Columbus left the colonists with their mines, while he continued his voyage among the other islands. Before he had seen all that he intended to see there, his crew grew so discontented that he went back to Hispaniola, only to find worse discontentment there. Many of the colonists had gone back to Spain, angry that they had found no gold, and that the natives did not remain friendly. They blamed Columbus for both these disappointments, and went home to complain of him to the king and queen. Columbus followed them as soon as possible, and found Ferdinand and Isabella still his friends. They promised to send him on a third voyage, but the preparations were delayed time after time, and Columbus saw that interest in his discovery was dying out. "The new-found world was thought to be a very poor India, after all."

It is said that a crowd called after the sons of Columbus, "Look at the sons of the Admiral of Mosquitoland, the man who has discovered the lands of deceit and disappointment!"

THE THIRD VOYAGE.

Columbus himself was not disheartened. He raised a new fleet. In May, 1498, he sailed again. This voyage took him to the mainland for the first time—the mainland of South America. Still he thought it India. He also visited his islands again. At Hayti, his brother Diego was in command of a fortified colony, but that, too, was a colony of disappointed gold-seekers. When Columbus arrived there both he and Diego were seized, put in chains, and sent to Spain as prisoners. In Spain and the colonies, too, by this time, the great admiral had many jealous enemies who made charges against him before the king and queen. But Ferdinand and Isabella and every one at court were sorry to see their great sea-hero in such distress. The king offered to grant the admiral almost any request. Columbus most desired to go out to his West Indies again, with full powers as governor, or to lead his promised crusade to Jerusalem. Neither of these requests could the king grant, but he could send the admiral to add to his discoveries.

COLUMBUS ON DECK.

THE FOURTH VOYAGE.

With a new fleet, Columbus started on his last expedition in May, 1502. This time he touched at what we call Central America. Honduras was discovered by the help of a rough map of the main shore, made by an old Indian whom Columbus took on board with him. On this voyage the admiral was ill, but his men carried his bed to the deck so that he could see the country and could send his men ashore in likely places. How happy he must have been when they told him that Honduras was a rich and beautiful country where the natives wore gold on their necks. Along that coast he sailed southward, till only the little strip of country, which you see on your map, separated the discoverers from the great Pacific Ocean whose farthest waves washed his desired India. He followed the coast of this neck, which we call Panama, turned eastward as it joined the southern continent, and then left it to return to the island colonies.

Columbus was then in deep distress. He was ill, his ships were worm-eaten and out of repair. He and his crews needed many things. He appealed to the colonists to relieve him; but they were indifferent and stingy. He wrote to his king: "I was twenty-eight years old when I came into your

Highnesses' service, and now I have not a hair upon me that is not grey; my body is infirm, and all that was left to me, as well as to my brothers, has been taken away and sold, even to the frock which I wore. . . . I cannot but believe that this was done without your royal permission."

LONELY DAYS IN SPAIN.

At length, in the autumn of 1504, the discoverer of the New World sailed back to Spain for the last time.

There all was changed. Queen Isabella was dead. Ferdinand was occupied with many cares. The great admiral was too ill to present himself at court, and the court left him alone in his trouble. Columbus watched and waited for some signs of favor until, after about two years, he died. That was in 1506. We do not know where he was buried. With him, during his last, sad days, was his son Diego, who had once been a page in the king's palace. No doubt he was proud of his father, even though the old sea-hero was dying broken-hearted. How much prouder he would have been if he had known all Columbus had achieved!

Much of the trouble which Columbus had to suffer he had brought upon himself by telling such extravagant stories of his discoveries that people who risked their lives and spent all their fortunes to go out to the new lands were bitterly disappointed. It is said that he was harsh with his sailors and colonists. But in those days nearly all story-tellers were extravagant and nearly all commanders were harsh. Columbus's discovery was the most glorious event of his time. Many mean persons were jealous of him, and they injured his fame. Perhaps they helped to turn the favor of the king against him; but if you read the history of Spain in those days, you will see that Ferdinand had a great many serious things to think of beside the admiral, for whom he had done so much and whose discoveries had cost the kingdom many fortunes, but had not led to the riches of India or Cathay.

You sometimes hear people say it is unjust that the New World was not named for Columbus; but it was not thought of as a new country until after Columbus was dead. He, and everyone of his time, believed that he had found merely the coast of India.

CHAPTER VII.

PIONEERS OF THE NORTHERN CONTINENT, 1000–1400.

Norsemen are said to have visited the northern continent of the New World long before Columbus discovered the West Indies. The Norsemen were bold sailors from the northern parts of Europe. They followed the sea as pirates, and were called vikings, not because they were kings, but because they made their headquarters in the deep viks or bays on the northern coast. Their songs, called sagas, tell of their voyages to a beautiful land, where they saw grapes in plenty and self-sown wheat. We do not know that they came to the shores of America, but many people believe that they did. They were venturesome voyagers. They certainly went from Norway to Iceland, from Iceland to Greenland, and from Greenland to Vinland. No one really knows just where Vinland was, but most people think it was somewhere along the New England coast. Sometimes they sailed into unknown waters to see what new land they could find. Oftener, their frail ships were blown to strange shores by the heavy winds of the north Atlantic.

They believed that all the places they visited were some new parts of Europe. That was not strange, for their own country, which they called Scandinavia, was a peninsula of Europe far from the mainland and cut into many parts by broad bays and rivers.

JOHN CABOT, ENGLAND'S PIONEER,
1497.

England claims that the northern continent was discovered by John Cabot, under the flag of King Henry VII. This Cabot, like Columbus, was born in Genoa. For many years he was a citizen of Venice, a beautiful city on the eastern coast of Italy, where many merchant-sailors lived and carried on an immense trade in the Mediterranean and Atlantic ports as far as England. From Venice, Cabot went to England, where he lived with his wife and sons in the famous seaport of Bristol. He was a skilled navigator, well taught in the geography of those days. He was one of the few men who believed, as Columbus did, in the roundness of the earth.

The news of the first voyage of Columbus made Cabot wish to follow up his countryman's discovery as soon as possible. Bristol is on the Atlantic side of England, and we can imagine that "the

Venetian," as he was called, often stood upon the shore, looking out on the ocean, impatient to be the next to give Europe news of its waves touching India. In March, 1497, before the great admiral's third expedition was ready, Cabot, and probably some of his merchant friends in Bristol, had equipped the ship *Mathew* for a voyage, under the king's authority. Henry VII. put no money into the enterprise, but he gave his commission, or patent, "unto John Cabot and his three sonnes, Lewis, Sebastian and Sancius, . . . for the discoverie of new and unknown lands." His majesty was to receive, "in wares or money, the fifth part of the capital gain so gotten."

THE DISCOVERY OF CAPE BRETON.

The little *Mathew* had a long voyage; but, June 24, 1497, she came to land. Some think that Cape Breton Island was the first part of the coast Cabot saw, and that he explored the Gulf of St. Lawrence. Others say that he entered Hudson's Bay. Be this as it may, the English claim that he crossed the north Atlantic, saw land, and returned to Bristol after about three months. In August, a Venetian, living in London at that time, wrote to his brother in Venice:

"Our countryman, who went, with a ship from

Bristol, in quest of new islands, is returned. . . . The king has promised that in the spring he shall have ten ships (armed to his order). . . . The king has also given him money, wherewith to amuse himself till then, and he is now at Bristol, with his wife, who is also Venetian, and with his sons: his name is Juan Cabot, and he is styled the great admiral. Vast honour is paid him: he dresses in silk, and these English run after him like mad people, so that he can enlist as many of them as he pleases. . . . The discoverer of these places planted on his newfound land a large cross, with one flag of England and another of St. Mark, by reason of his being a Venetian, so that our banner has floated very far afield."

Cabot, like Columbus, thought he had found the eastern coast of Asia. Of course every one in Europe thought so, too. Another Italian wrote from London to Milan, a city in Italy:

"Perhaps . . . it may not displease you to learn how his Majesty here has won a part of Asia without a stroke of the sword. The said Master John, as being foreign-born and poor, would not be believed if his comrades, who are almost all Englishmen and from Bristol, did not testify that what he says is true. This Master John has the description of the world in a chart and also in a solid globe, which he has made . . . : they affirm that the sea is covered with fishes, which are caught not only with the net but with baskets, a stone being tied to them, in order that the baskets may sink into water . . But Master John has set his mind on something greater: for he expects to go farther on toward the east from that place already occupied, constantly hugging the shore, until he shall be over against an island by him called Cipango, where he thinks all the spices of the world, and also the precious stones, originate."

CABOT'S SECOND VOYAGE.

It is said that Cabot, or his son Sebastian, made another voyage with a fleet furnished by the King in the next year, and that the mainland was then discovered; that they coasted for many miles along the shores of New England.

Both Columbus and Cabot would have been sorry to know that they had not found India, but, instead, new continents peopled by savages who were in no way related to the skilful silk-weavers and jewel-workers of India.

AMERIGO VESPUCCI,
1497 or 1499 1512.

The new country was to be named after Amerigo Vespucci, a man who was deeply interested in the great admiral's voyages, and wanted to cross the ocean himself as soon as possible. Some say that he sailed so soon that he was the first to see the southern continent, in 1497.

Vespucci was born in Florence, not very far from Genoa. Among the many stories of his life is one which describes him in Seville, employed by the men who fitted out the ships of Columbus for a third voyage. A letter of his own, written some time later, tells that he was far away from Spain at that time. It says that he was returning home from the West Indies on a voyage for Ferdinand and Isabella, in which he had found the coast of the southern continent near the mouth of the Orinoco River. If that is true, Amerigo Vespucci and neither Columbus nor Cabot was the first European to find the mainland of the New World. There is no account of this voyage in the public records of Spain. Later, in 1499, however, Vespucci was pilot for Ojeda, a Spaniard who visited Trinidad the same year that Columbus saw that island.

Some time after that, this Florentine voyager wrote an interesting little book, which was an account of his four journeys to the " New Land."

THE LAND IS CALLED AMERICA.

In 1507 a new geography was made at the University of St.-Dié, a little town in the Vosges mountains near the river Rhine. In the back of the new geography were copies of Vespucci's letters on his four journeys. The learned doctor who made the geography called attention to the letters and how much they added to the Europeans' knowledge of the world.

He said: "Now truly, as these regions are more widely explored and another fourth part is discovered by Americus Vesputius, as may be learned from the following letters, I see no reason why it should not justly be called 'America.'"

All Europe was interested in the additions which had been made to the knowledge of the world. There was much interest, also, in the new style of books printed from type. That wonderful little new geography, from the university town in the mountains between France and Germany, must have had a large circulation for its day. The people who read it liked the learned doctor's suggestion of giving the new land a name of its own. So, without the aid of Vespucci, or even his knowledge, perhaps, all Europe began to talk of America.

Amerigo waked one day to find himself famous. The king of Spain made him "pilot-major" of the kingdom. People talked to him and about him and of his wonderful discoveries.

Florence was delighted that such a great man

AMERIGO VESPUCCI.

should be a Florentine. This is a picture of a statue raised there in his honor. There were people who did not believe that he had told the truth, and who thought it was wrong to give his name to the new-found parts of India. Perhaps they were jealous, perhaps they honestly thought so.

Whether Amerigo deserved to have a continent named for him or not, is still undecided. After all, you will agree that you like the name of America and that you can admire Columbus and Cabot just as much, if your native country does not bear their names.

WHAT ATTRACTED OTHER PIONEERS.

After the New World was discovered at the close of the fifteenth century, what do you think attracted thousands of adventurers to it during the sixteenth century? The motives for voyages of discovery in this century were many and varied; so were the attractions the new country contained.

The sailors of the Levant, who were the ablest seamen of Europe in that day, seemed suddenly to have outgrown the Mediterranean Sea. Voyages to England, and down the west coast of Africa, seemed to be child's play, when men and ships could breast the high waves of the Atlantic, and come back, not only alive, but with wild Indians, strange animals, brilliant birds, and many other curiosities. Moreover, every one believed that the new land contained untold treasures, and that the riches of India and Cathay lay not far from the coast.

A SEPARATE CONTINENT.

Before this sixteenth century was half over they learned that South America, at least, was a land wholly separate from the Orient. Then they grew only the more confident that India must lie but a short distance beyond. The great object was to find the strait which led across the New World to the Old. In that quest the explorers found much that they were not looking for. Within the first half century after the discovery, the people of Europe thought they knew a great deal about America. Of the southern continent much was known, because the Spaniards went there with small armies, and conquered the native peoples of Mexico, Peru, and Brazil.

The northern continent had no such great nations to conquer. The armies that went there were lost in thickets and swamps. The people of Europe talked of Florida and Norumbega, of Canada, Hochelaga, and the New Found Land, in the most vague way, not knowing much about their position or boundaries.

HOW GLORY WAS WON IN AMERICA.

The vast amount of land, and the possibilities of all it might contain, attracted hundreds of explorers to risk their lives. To face danger was an honor in those days, especially to go out into unknown danger. It was an honor, also, to plant a king's standard in a strange land, and to claim the right to add a big piece of even unexplored territory to a royal dominion. Kings and queens rewarded such service, as it was called, with titles of nobility, with large tracts of the new dominion, and often with large powers as governor over colonies there. The proudest man in those days was he who went to his sovereign with the most marvelous stories about America, and of his own prowess in conquering the natives for the glory of his king and his religion.

A FRENCHMAN'S DESCRIPTION.

One of the French explorers of this time wrote a long letter about what he saw. He said:

"We entered and viewed the country, which is the fairest, fruitfulest, and pleasantest of all the world, abounding in honey, wax, venison, wild fowl, forests, woods of all sorts, palm-trees, cypresses, cedars, bays, the highest and greatest, with also the fairest vines in all the world, with

SOUTH AMERICA.

grapes according, which naturally, without art or man's help or trimming, will grow to tops of oaks and other trees that be of wonderful greatness and height. . . . Also there are silkworms in marvelous number, a great deal fairer and better than our silkworms.

"The natives showed us by signs that they had in the land gold and silver and copper, whereof we have brought some home."

How much of this account was true we shall find out as we go on with our stories. Then it was all believed and constantly repeated.

The kings took as great an interest in these things as did the people. If Spain was increasing her dominion, England must do the like, and so must France. So the rivalry of kings spurred on the explorers.

VERRAZANO,
1524.

France, as well as Spain and England, sent an Italian navigator to the New World. This was Verrazano, a Florentine like Amerigo Vespucci. You can remember that the two C's were born in Genoa, and the two V's in Florence. Verrazano had been a brave seaman under the French flag for many years before King Francis I. heard of his daring on the Spanish Main. All of Spain's enemies in those days sent out armed vessels to capture her treasure-ships on their way home from their conquests in South America. That part of the Atlantic sailed by these treasure-ships was called the Spanish Main.

When Francis I. saw Spain and England laying their claims to America, he said he should like to see France take a share; and when he heard of the bold and skilful corsair, Verrazano, his majesty sent for him at once. The king gave him the *Dauphin*, with fifty men, and food and provisions for eight months, and told him to take possession of some part of the New World in the name of France.

Verrazano left France in 1524. He reached our coast near Cape Fear, in what is now North Carolina. First he sailed southward, as near the shore as possible, in search of a good harbor; but finding nothing to suit him, he returned and went northward. Then he explored what we know as Raleigh Bay, New York Harbor and Newport Harbor, and many other places, until he reached Cape Breton. From there he sailed back to France. England claimed that the Cabots had explored this coast, or part of it; but they showed no maps till fifty years after the Cabot voyage. Verrazano was the first to make it known to Europe. On board the *Dauphin* he wrote a letter to Francis I., in which he described the waters and the lands he had visited, the people, their dress and manners, and many other things besides. He believed that vast treasure was to be found inland.

The letter has been criticized ever since it was written, three centuries and a half ago. Some people have always doubted the truth of the statements; but they have never been disproved. Verazano's letter was an inspiration to young navigators for nearly a century, and it is quoted to this day by the most learned writers on America. Many of the interesting things about the early Indians which you have read in this book are taken from it.

With the exception of an attempt at settlement near the mouth of the Mississippi River, and one in South Carolina at Port Royal, France put her energy into colonizing the region to the north about the St. Lawrence River, where the prospects were good for fur trade, and about Nova Scotia, where the fisheries would well repay any efforts.

In 1534 Jacques Cartier had attempted a settlement at Montreal, and another at Quebec in 1541. Although these were not permanent, they proved to be germs of later colonies. Champlain founded a settlement, in 1608, at Quebec, which grew and flourished. About the banks of New Newfoundland the French fishermen had gathered from the very beginning of the sixteenth century. In the early years of the seventeenth century they built a Port Royal in what the English called Nova Scotia.

WHAT THE PIONEERS ACCOMPLISHED.

Before we leave the early voyagers, who explored the shores of both North and South America on both the eastern and western sides, let us stop to see a little of what they accomplished.

Columbus, the great pioneer and daring sailor, proved that the earth was round, and gave courage to hundreds to follow him.

Vespucci gained more exact knowledge, and furnished a name for the new land.

Verrazano secured to the French a claim which gave impulse to the great French pioneers, Jacques Cartier and Champlain.

Pizarro, Coronado, Balboa and Cortez gave the most thrilling accounts of a richer and more civilized people than any others had found in the New World.

While Spain was still in hopes of finding more rich cities and treasure, her soldiers and priests had established missions among the Pueblos. You will remember where these people lived and about their old houses. In the very centre of the Pueblo region Santa Fé was settled, and in time the missions stretched in a long chain to the Gulf of California on the Pacific coast.

Before the middle of the sixteenth century many hundreds of Spanish soldiers and colonists held South and Central America. Pizarro had won vast amounts of treasure and gold in Peru, and Cortez in Mexico. After that it was for treasure that Spanish kings sent Spanish soldiers to America. Their motto was "To the South for gold." This led them to turn away from the northern country, where the fur trade in time would have brought them wealth, and from the fields where Indian corn might be raised by hard and constant work.

The old records tell of many Spanish forts and missions, started in what is now the United States; and how several French settlements were destroyed by the Spaniards. The oldest town in our country is of their building. That is St. Augustine, which was settled in 1565.

Many daring English sailors visited North America in the sixteenth century. Hawkins, Drake, Gilbert and Frobisher roved the seas and explored the coasts, while Richard Hakluyt, at home, gathered carefully all accounts of their voyages and discoveries, compared their reports and gains with those of Spanish and French discoverers, and besought his queen, Elizabeth, at the close of the sixteenth century, to begin to settle the new land with colonies of English people.

CHAPTER VIII.

INDIANS AND EUROPEANS.

Picture to yourselves an Indian, standing on a hill above the beach of any part of our Atlantic shore that you know best. It is early morning. The Indian is looking intently at a strange vessel, which is many, many times larger than his largest bark canoe or any quintan he has ever hollowed from the trunk of a big tree. It has tall sticks standing on the deck, with pieces of white cloth hanging from them. It seems to move toward him, yet no one is seen using paddles.

The white cloths drop. Over the bow is lowered a big, black thing, which looks in the distance like a heavy imitation of a sprung bow and arrow. After that is dropped into the water, some boats are seen. They are more like canoes, but larger and broader. In each there are several white-skinned men, their bodies covered with cloth that fits them—a very strange sight, far different from Indians dressed in skins and blankets. These men sit in their boats and use many paddles that stick out on both sides in an unheard-of way; but they

Discovery of Hispaniola (from Herrera).

move swiftly over the water. They run upon the beach and come ashore.

PLANTING THE KING'S STANDARD.

Other natives, men and women, have seen the sight, and gather to meet the strangers as they leave their boats. The natives look with delight on these people, whose faces are of so much lighter color than their own, and whose bodies are closely covered with gay-colored stuffs and with armor that shines in the morning sunlight. Many interesting things are in their hands, too. The natives think that these beings are gods, who have come to be worshiped. So, in fear and reverence, the red-skins keep together and watch the leader of the visitors, as he takes his stand on some high point of ground above the beach and plants a cross in the name of his king and church, while the men stand by, with their hats off, and the devout soldier priests, in their black and white robes, read a solemn service.

The natives cannot understand what they see, but they watch it all intently. When the strangers have finished their ceremony, they come toward the natives, holding out to them bright-colored bells, mirrors, and other wonderful things, which the natives finally take in their own hands and examine with delight. When they hand them back to the visitors they are told in sign language to keep them. That fills them with greater delight, and they are soon very friendly, showing the strangers how they live and trying to tell them all that they wish to know.

WHAT THE STRANGERS SEE.

The leader of the white men is deeply interested in all that he sees. He visits the fields where grows a grain that is new to him. It grows in little hills, set in rows. The plant is tall, has long, rustling leaves, and the grain grows in kernels on a cob that is covered with husks and has a long, silky tassel at the top. The natives call it maize. White men have called it Indian corn. The Indians give the leader bread made of this corn, which he finds good. They give him fruit from their trees, too, and potatoes, the root of a plant. Then they invite him to smoke their pipes filled with a plant they raise, which we call tobacco. There are many new and beautiful trees and bushes and wild flowers, but the leader can stop only a short time in each place where he plants his king's standard. He soon gives a signal to his men. They go down to the beach and make ready the boats to return to the vessel. But some are at other business.

STEALING NATIVES.

The Indians hear a cry from one of their young girls. They see her struggling between two strong men who carry her down to a boat and push off quickly. In another boat is one of their young men, trying to leap out, but uttering no cry, lest he seem cowardly.

The natives' wonder and delight is changed to anger and to fear. Some run to their huts for their bows and arrows. Others get out their quintans; but the strangers have reached their ship and are sailing away with their captives before the indignant natives can attack them. There is nothing to do but angrily to watch the white sails out of sight, and then to hold rude, but sad ceremonies to express their loss and grief. They cherish their rage. They watch for white men's ships, with weapons ready to kill any who may try to land.

THE NATIVES IN EUROPE.

The early explorers seldom went back to Europe without a few natives. In all the great cities the Indians were the wonders of their time. If they were chiefs or the children of chiefs they were sometimes treated as royal.

They were shown at court. Their portraits

were painted. They were often carefully taught many things to convert them to the Christian religion and to civilization. After a few years, many of them were taken back to teach their people and to help the white men plant colonies; but many who returned were landed hundreds of miles from their homes.

The natives who walked the streets, marveling at all they saw in Europe, little knew how much their visits had to do with the planting of white men's colonies in their native land.

REASONS FOR PLANTING COLONIES.

Some Europeans who saw the natives and heard that they worshiped the sun, moon and stars, began at once to plan to send missionaries to teach them the Christian religion. The Roman Catholics of Spain and France spread their missions far and wide. They altered, if they did not entirely change, the beliefs of all the northern and southern Indians.

In England, many people desired to send Protestant missionaries to the middle regions. One of these, you have heard, was Richard Hakluyt, a clergyman, who made a book for Englishmen, to tell them all that was known about the New World in other countries of Europe. Hakluyt urged his queen, Elizabeth, to plant " one or two colonies of our nation upon that fyrme," or land, " where they may first learn the language of the people . . . and by little and little acquainte themselves with their manners, and distill into their mynds the swete and lively liquor of the gospel."

TRADE.

Merchants who saw the Indians had other desires which led them to fit out colonies. They thought of the many things they could sell in the New World. Hakluyt helped them, too. He said: " All savages will take marvelous delight in any garment, be it ever so simple: as a shirt, a blue, yellow, red, or green cotton cassacke, a cap, or such like, and will take incredible pains for such a trifle." It was soon well known how the Indians delighted in beads, bells, and other trinkets. For such cheap trifles they were willing to exchange precious metals and jewels, if they had them, and large quantities of furs and woods, which brought high prices in Europe.

Many statesmen thought it would be a piece of economy to take the prisoners out of the prisons, where they lived in idleness and cost the government a great deal of money, and to set them at work in America to build up a great colony, which should supply the London merchants with furs and other valuable things.

ROYAL RIVALRY.

There was a still stronger reason urged upon Queen Elizabeth to send out colonies to North America. Whenever a king of Europe made a good claim to any part of the New World, his power became greater in the Old World. The queen was advised to favor some action, lest, "by our slackness, we suffer the French, or others, to prevent us."

Before the close of the sixteenth century the pioneers from Europe to America had begun to see that a cross in the New World and a royal proclamation in the Old World were not enough to secure a sovereign's claim to the discoveries made in his name. Discoveries must be confirmed by settlements.

We shall see that all these reasons and plans worked together when, at last, at the opening of the seventeenth century, England made a permanent settlement in the New World.

CHAPTER IX.

FIRST SETTLEMENTS IN VIRGINIA.

In Queen Elizabeth's time several companies of English colonists tried to make settlements on the coast somewhere north of the Spanish settlements in Florida. England claimed all the country north of the Spanish settlement, and called it Virginia, in honor of Elizabeth, their Virgin Queen.

The first people who came as colonists faced dangers and endured great suffering. They were sent out, with the queen's permission, by Sir Humphrey Gilbert, Sir Walter Raleigh, and generous men who joined them, and gave their fortunes, and sometimes their lives, to plant an English commonwealth in the New World.

THE FIRST ENGLISH CHILD BORN IN AMERICA.

One of the early colonies which did not succeed settled on Roanoke Island, in what is now Albemarle Sound; and there a little girl was born. She was Virginia Dare, the first child of English parents born in America. Possibly she grew up with the Indians, but not there at Roanoke. Her grandfather, John White, left her and the colony, with

all going well, to get supplies from England; but
the next English captain who went there found
that everyone was gone and the houses were in
ruins. Sir Walter Raleigh and his friends searched
for them for years; but no one ever found trace of
them. They may have perished from hunger.
They may have tried to go back to England in
some frail boat of their own. Spaniards or Indians
may have killed or captured them. Wild beasts
may have devoured them. We know how all of
these misfortunes destroyed other colonies; but no
one knows what ruined the first settlement at
Roanoke.

NEW VENTURES.

By 1607 the queen was dead, Raleigh was in
prison, and English people had learned that one or
two men could not afford to send out colonies at so
heavy a cost. Then a large number of men decided
to form a company to undertake this work of colony
planting. You remember that the country had
rich forests, fertile soil, abundance of animals for
food and furs; and that everyone felt sure that there
were mines of gold besides. The new companies
decided to send out regular trading agents and
workmen bound to serve them for a certain number of years, on much the same plan that the great
East India Company of England had adopted to set

up stations or "factories," through the country and keep agents or colonies in charge of them. The East India Company had grown rich and powerful, and some of the members thought they also would make a great success of the Virginia Company.

JAMESTOWN.

One day in April, in the year 1607, the *Susan Constant*, the *Good Speed* and the *Discovery* sailed

into the Chesapeake Bay. For a few days the men who came in these ships explored the shores about there, then decided to settle upon a peninsula, about fifty miles up a river which was called the James, in honor of their king, James of England.

There was much hard work to do, much danger to face and suffering to bear, before this settlement or plantation, as they called it, was established, but it was finally secured—the first permanent English settlement in America. There were about one hundred men in the three ships. Some of them were "gentlemen," who had never done any work. Others came for adventure, to find gold, to see the new country, and to have a good time. Besides, there were about twelve mechanics and a few strong men of good sense, who knew how much work was to be done, and that each man must be industrious, obey orders, and do his part.

Captain Newport was in command of the largest ship, the *Susan Constant*. He was in charge of the entire expedition until it reached Virginia. King James I. had given him a sealed box, which contained a list of such men of the party as his Majesty had selected to form a council to govern the colony. This box was not to be opened until they made their land-fall. Imagine how curious they must have been to see these names during their long voyage. After the box was opened and the king's instructions were read, all the men named with one exception were sworn into the council. Captain John Smith was deprived of his share in the government for about a month. Then he, too, was sworn into office. This council elected for their chairman or president a rich merchant of London, whose name, Edward Maria Wingfield, you may think rather odd. The peninsula chosen for Jamestown was low and malarious. The colonists were not the sort of men to work willingly, even for food.

THE COMMON-STORE SYSTEM.

There was trouble from the beginning. All the colonists were bound by an agreement with the company in England to live and to work on what was called the common-store system for seven years. All the game and fish that were taken, all the corn that was received from the Indians or raised by the colonists, all the food that they brought with them, or might obtain in any way, was put into a common store-house.

Out of that the treasurer of the colony, or Cape Marchant, gave equal portions to all the colonists. When there was more than they needed it was to be sold to the merchants, and the proceeds sent to the company in England. In the same way the lumber that the colonists cut, the furs and other things they received from the Indians, and all that they could raise for market, were put into the common store, and sent to the company by Captain Newport, who sailed back and forth regularly. By this plan no man had the results of his own labor. The possibility of a share in a general settlement, seven years hence, seemed a small reward. Many would not try to work. Some of these were willing to hunt for gold and gems, which no one ever found in Virginia.

HELP FROM THE INDIANS.

Several of the colonists wrote letters and books about these early days in Jamestown. Wingfield tells how, in June, "an Indian came from the great Powhatan with the word of peace; that he desired greatly our friendship . . . that we should sow and reap in peace. . . . A little after this came a deer to the President from the Great Powhatan. He and his messengers were pleased with trifles. The President likewise bought deer of the Indians, beavers and other flesh, which he always caused to be equally divided among the colony."

From malaria and hunger there was such sickness in Jamestown that nearly half of the colony died before September. Another writer said: "We lived for the space of five months in this miserable distress . . . as yet we had no houses to cover us, our tents were rotten, and our cabins worse than nought."

CAPTAIN JOHN SMITH AND POWHATAN.

The man who wrote this about the tents and cabins was Captain John Smith. He had come with the others, and was one of the king's council. After a time he was made president. Smith was one of the few men of the colony who was always ready to work—to build cabins, or fish, or hunt, or to help make the log palisade around the settlement. He often took small parties of settlers into the Indians' country, to buy corn, and to carry out the company's orders to explore the rivers and the bay. He gave the natives beads, pieces of copper and hatchets for their corn. He was so strong and

CAPTAIN JOHN SMITH.

brave with them, too, when they threatened to attack the white men, that they feared and respected him and became good friends to the colony as long as he stayed in Jamestown.

On one of Captain Smith's first visits to Powhatan's country, the great chief's brother captured the white man and his party, and threatened to kill them. But, by appearing not to be afraid, and by telling tales to interest and amuse the Indian Emperor, Smith turned his captivity into a pleasant visit, from which he went home laden with presents. This is an account of the visit, with the captain's spelling changed to ours.

MAKING FRIENDS OF ENEMIES.

"Arriving at Werannocomoco, their Emperor . . . kindly welcomed me with good words and great platters of sundry victuals, assuring me of his friendship and my liberty within four days." Powhatan "admired and was not a little feared" when Smith told him "of the great king of England, of the territories of Europe which were subject to him, and of the innumerable multitude of his ships, the noise of trumpets and terrible manner of fighting," which the king's subject would use here in Virginia if necessary.

Powhatan desired the colony to forsake Paspahegh, as he called the region about Jamestown, and to live with him upon his river.

"He promised to give me corn, venison, or what I wanted to feed us, hatchets and copper we should make him, and none should disturb us. This request I promised to perform, and thus having, with all the kindness he could devise, sought to content me, he sent me home with four men, one that usually carried my gown and knapsack after me, two others loaded with bread, and one to accompany me."

PRESIDENT WINGFIELD.

The poor Jamestown settlers often provoked trouble with the natives. They quarreled among themselves and with President Wingfield, too. Perhaps he was not as wise nor strong nor as kind as he might have been, yet he said he tried hard to be fair with what belonged to all, and generous with what was his own. But, at length, the council put him out of office, sent him on board one of the boats in the harbor and kept him there as a prisoner. In writing his complaint in later years, Wingfield said: "It is further said I did much banquet and ryot. I never had but one squirrell roasted, whereof I gave part to Mr. Ratcliff, then sick; yet was that squirrell given to me."

MORE COLONISTS.

In the spring of 1608 Captain Newport arrived from England again with a new party of better men, who gave fresh courage to all. He put his men at work to build a new storehouse and a church, "all which workes they finished cheerfully." Then he went up the river with his ship and came back with it well loaded with corn, wheat, beans and peas. Newport also induced the colonists to allow Wingfield to come on shore to sleep until the deposed president went back to England with him.

In the autumn of 1608 a third party of colonists came to Jamestown, with some women and children. As soon as family life began, the colony grew happier and stronger.

A NEW GOVERNMENT.

A new charter was given to the company in England in 1609. By it the company was able to make some changes toward better government in the colony. In place of a president, chosen by the local council, there was to be a governor chosen by their council in England. The governor had authority from the king and the company, and nearly all Englishmen of that day thought no authority was of any power unless it came from the king. The colony was still to live and work on their common-store system.

SMITH'S DEPARTURE.

This same year of 1609 the company sent five hundred new emigrants to Jamestown. Some of them arrived before the new governor. Captain John Smith very soon after this went back to England either, as he said, on account of his wounded arm, or, as others believed, because the company recalled him. He went back, leaving the colony in charge of a gentleman named George Percy, who was a good man, but in poor health. When Smith left, Jamestown had "a church, a fort, a storehouse, sixty dwelling-houses, and a stock of domestic animals." Besides, there were fields and several plantations outside of the town.

As soon as the captain was gone, all the colonists, old and new, refused to work. When the Indians heard that their friend had left, and how badly the colonists behaved without him, they attacked the settlers and destroyed their property almost to the very gates of Jamestown. Within a year the colony dwindled to sixty persons. They were just going away when another load of fresh colonists, with plenty of supplies, came with the governor, Lord de la War, whose name we call Delaware.

The governor set everyone to work, and built the settlement up again; but he was soon forced to go back to England for his health. Then the colonists resumed their lazy ways, and almost perished again.

CHAPTER X.

HOW THE PLANTATION OF VIRGINIA WAS SAVED BY DALE.

In less than a year after Governor De la War left Jamestown, it was almost in ruins for the second or third time. That was in 1611. The man who saved it was Sir Thomas Dale. He came as High Marshal of Virginia. He remained about five years. After that the fear of failure was passed. Dale was soon followed by three hundred more colonists. One hundred cows and other cattle were soon sent by the company. He was a second Captain Smith. "All the men in the colony either worked or starved while he was governor." He began a new and healthy plantation not far from Jamestown, which was called, for Prince Henry, the City of Henrico.

Dale also induced the company to begin carefully to alter the common-store system. A few colonists were allowed to have three acres each, and to work for themselves upon this land. The change was so successful that it was extended, and finally the old system was abandoned.

SOME STRICT LAWS.

Before this change was made, however, Dale had to give orders and enforce them to make each man do his share. In order to increase the number of poultry, Dale made a rule that no person was to kill a domestic fowl, whether it was his own or not. No baker nor cook who was supposed to work for the common store should ask for pay or keep back any of the food. If he did he was to have his ears cut off. These rules and many others were read by the minister in church each Sunday morning. This was a disagreeable duty, because the minister knew how the people disliked the rules, or "Dale's Code," as they were called; but he knew that if he did not read them he would not receive his full share of the next week's food.

BETTER DAYS IN JAMESTOWN.

The people in Jamestown did not need such strict laws after a while, for a better class of men began to come over from England, to grow rich by raising tobacco. Governor Yeardley, who took Sir Thomas Dale's place in 1616, advised the cultivation of this plant, for which there was a growing demand in Europe. The temptation was then strong to raise tobacco rather than corn, each man leaving that for his neighbor to do. The more sensible men in the colony remedied this by passing a law that every man must have on hand an amount of corn in proportion to the number of men employed by him.

Meanwhile the Indians were friendly, especially the great chief, Powhatan. His daughter had to be kidnapped, however, to bring this about.

THE KIDNAPPING OF POCAHUNTAS.

"Powhatan's delight and darling, his daughter, Pocahuntas, . . . tooke some pleasure . . . to be among her friends at Patoamecke." These are lines from a true story, written by Raphe Hamor in Virginia, in 1614, and printed soon after in England. That year, 1614, Powhatan's delight and darling left her home, to see something of her friends, when her father sent down a party of his men with corn and furs to sell to the settlers. At that time the great chief was holding some of the colonists in captivity. He had also obtained possession of some valuable swords and guns. In vain had Dale asked the stern old Indian "Emperor" to give them up. It was feared that the men would be killed.

It chanced that at this time Captain Argall, a daring sort of English trader, was on one of his frequent visits to Virginia, and had sailed up the

"Potoamecke." Argall thought it would be much to his credit to discover some means to force Powhatan to give up the men and the guns.

What do you think he did? He induced an Indian, named Japazeus, to help him kidnap Pocahuntas, not to hurt her, but to take her down to Jamestown and keep her with the settlers until her father gave up their men and the swords and guns. One day when Japazeus and his wife and Pocahuntas were walking on the shore, the wife proposed to pay a visit to Captain Argall's boat, which lay in the river. An English boat was an interesting thing to visit, she told Pocahuntas, and she finally persuaded the young girl to go with her. Everything on board was ready to receive them. Pocahuntas was somewhat afraid at first; but she soon took delight in the boat and all she saw. A supper was served, and then the Princess was made comfortable for the night in the gunner's room.

In the morning she rose early, to tell Japazeus that she wished to go back to the shore. Captain Argall had provided for this. He had "secretly well rewarded Japazeus with a small copper kettle" and some other toys, which he valued so highly that "doubtless he would have betraide his owne father for them." "Much a doe there was to perswade her to be patient." This " with extraordinary curteous usage, by little and little," was done, and "so to Jamestowne she was brought." A messenger was sent forthwith to her father to say that his only daughter was in the hands of the English until he fulfilled their conditions for her return. "The news was unwelcome and troublesome unto him, partly for the love he bare to his daughter, and partly for the love he bare to our men, his prisoners, of whom . . . he made great use; and those swords and peeces [or guns] of ours, which, though of no use to him, it delighted him to view and looke upon."

A HAPPY VISIT.

Many months passed while Pocahuntas lived at the fort, or on board Argall's boat. The English boys and girls were happy to be her playmates. All the people loved her and still treated her as a princess, and she loved them.

Powhatan made several offers to do part of what Dale and the captain asked; but he refused to do all. Then the captain sailed up the river with Pocahuntas, to see if it would move the stubborn old chief to have his delight and darling so near, yet out of his reach. Two brothers of Pocahuntas came on board the boat one day, "being very desirous to see their sister." When they saw how well she was treated they were delighted, and rushed away to persuade their father to redeem Pocahuntas, and to make a firm peace forever with us."

THE LADY REBECCA AND HER MARRIAGE.

Meanwhile Pocahuntas was told that she was free to go to her father, if she wished to do so. But Master John Rolfe had fallen in love with her by this time, and she chose to go back to Jamestown and be married to him. When Powhatan heard of this he consented to the marriage, and made a treaty, agreeing to all the English asked of him. Pocahuntas went back to Jamestown with an uncle and two brothers. The uncle gave the little Indian bride away in the church at Jamestown on the 5th of April, 1614. " Ever since then," the story goes, " we have had friendly commerce and trade, not only with Powhatan, but also with all his subjects round about us."

Soon after the marriage Marshall Dale went back to England. With him sailed Mr. Rolfe and his Indian princess bride, who was baptized before her marriage under the name of the Lady Rebecca.

CHAPTER XI.

PLANTATION LIFE IN VIRGINIA.

You recall that after the settlers began to work for themselves they did not need such strict laws as "Dale's Code" to keep them at work. Another change in the company enabled them to give up the common-store system, to sell large tracts of land at low prices to what were called "planters." They gave these planters the right to elect delegates of their own to a legislature, or House of Burgesses, which met with the governor and his council in what they called a general assembly, and made the laws for the colony.

Then a better class of Englishmen began to think it worth while to come to Virginia to take up plantations of hundreds of acres. They raised tobacco on these plantations, and soon grew to like the colony so well that they built large, substantial houses, sent for their families, and called Virginia their home. The tobacco-fields of the large planters were laid out along the James River and its small branches, and along the bay. There were no cities in Virginia, although the company wished for them so much that a group of plantations was often called a city, and efforts were made to lay out a town as a centre for them.

Each plantation was a small settlement in itself. It had its own little harbor; ships came from England to its landing, bringing all the articles and provisions that were not made or raised on the plantation, and taking the planters' tobacco crop for return cargo. There was no need for towns with shops. There was little coin—tobacco was the currency of the colony. Its value was fixed by acts of the general assembly. There were one or two schools for poor white and Indian children. A few planters' children were taught at home until the boys were old enough to be sent to England for their education. People lived an out-of-door life—fox-hunting, horseback-riding, boating. They did not care much for colonial newspapers; printing was not allowed in their colony for over a hundred years. A planter's wealth was in his land and his servants, and in the large crops of tobacco which he sent to England to pay for supplies and luxuries.

NEGRO SLAVES.

In 1619, soon after the large landholders began to come to Virginia, something new was offered for sale at Jamestown. A Dutch ship offered some negroes, who had been stolen from the coast of Africa. The tobacco planters of the West Indies had used negroes as slaves for years, and the Dutch traders brought them to Virginia as soon as they heard of the new tobacco plantations. Others that came soon after found equally ready sale. But nearly thirty years passed before many such cargoes began to come. In these early days the tobacco was raised by white servants. Before the old common-store system was abolished all colonists were bound to one master—the company. After it was abolished, every planter was a master, who took servants under bonds, much as the company had done. A few of these were the worst sort of criminals from the English prisons, and were bound to the planters for life; but most of them were under bonds or indenture as

"FREE-WILLERS OR REDEMPTIONERS."

They were often good and industrious, even educated men, who had lost their farms, or had had other misfortunes in England, and wished to start anew in Virginia. So they bound themselves for a number of years to work for some large landowner, who paid their passage, kept them in food and clothes until the end of "their time," as they called their bondage. Then they received a certain number of acres, a small outfit of tools, and, perhaps, some money or goods, with which they set up small plantations of their own as "freedmen," or "redemptioners." Many of the honored families of Virginia were founded in this way.

DUTY-BOYS OR APPRENTICES.

Boys formed another class of white servants in the early days of the colony. They were bound much as the "free-willers." But they were often taken from England against their choice. Sometimes they were drugged and kidnapped by ship-captains, who received certain pay, called a bounty, on every servant they landed in Virginia.

The boys were sometimes of poor families; sometimes their parents were rich; but all shared about the same hard life in Virginia, and it usually lasted until the boy became of age.

PRISONER-SERVANTS.

The old plan, to send England's prison inmates to America, was carried out on a large scale in the important years following 1619. Some of these, you know, were criminals, bound for life as a mercy, instead of hanging them; but most of them were not vicious, and many had good characters. In those days a good man was often in prison because the king, some prince, or other great man, did not choose to keep up his friendship. The news that he had lost favor would spread. Any landlord or tailor, butcher or baker, who happened to have a debt against him, could keep him in prison until he paid it. In the same way, any upright man, who fell ill, or was overtaken by any misfortune, might be thrust into jail for the food he had used or the rent of the farm whose crops had failed. The jails were damp and dirty, and the prisoners often died before they could find any way to get out and work to pay their debts. It was a bad system, and has now been abolished. Such prisons, bad as they were, cost the kingdom much, and James I. thought it an excellent plan to send many ship-loads of the prisoners to Virginia, where planters were glad to have them. The ship-captains received money for each person they took over, the king or the company received something, too; the planter had the man's labor for five years, perhaps, and the prisoner worked out his liberty as an honest man, and became owner of a small plantation of his own.

THE INDIAN MASSACRE.

The last event of importance between the Indians and the pioneers of Virginia was the massacre of 1622.

After that disaster, the company did everything that could be done to restore the colony to strength at once. They sent help of all kinds and thousands of new colonists. From that time there was less trouble with the Indians. They fell back to the interior, and, although they occasionally broke out in hostilities, they were always quickly quelled after the great massacre. The early Indian life and the pioneer life of the plantation of Virginia disappeared.

In later years, during a struggle between opposing political parties in the colony, Jamestown was burned. You see its ruins in this picture, just as you may see them if you go there now, for the town was never rebuilt. It had done its work as the first permanent settlement in Virginia.

RUINS OF JAMESTOWN.

CHAPTER XII.

VIRGINIA'S NEIGHBORS.

The English were later than their rivals in beginning their colonization, but they had one decided advantage over them in the temperate climate of the region they chose. Their settlements suffered much from the new climate, but Virginia was favored with a less intense heat in summer than the region of Spanish plantations, and with a far milder winter than the French endured in the North. Upon the Chesapeake Bay the greater part of the year was warm, and the soil was so fertile that a moderate amount of industry in the tobacco-fields and the corn-fields was repaid with large crops.

MARYLAND, 1633.

To these warmer regions of the "corn belt," Lord Baltimore turned in 1621, from the colder coast of Nova Scotia, where he had been trying to settle a colony at Avalon. With his band of colonists, he sailed south to Virginia. There he was unwelcome, for both he and most of his colonists were Roman Catholics, while the Virginia colonists were stanch members of the Church of England.

After a short visit, Baltimore went back to England, and a few years later secured from Charles I., his king and friend, a grant of land to the north of Virginia. This was called Maryland, in honor of the king's wife, Henrietta Maria.

Like William Penn, the Quaker founder of Pennsylvania, Lord Baltimore wanted to make this large tract of land serve both as an asylum for his persecuted fellow-believers, and as a source of income to himself as proprietor. So he made it known that in Maryland Roman Catholics could freely believe and worship as they thought right. At the same time, in order to attract other colonists, he made wise provisions for toleration. In his letter of instructions to colonists, Lord Baltimore said: "Preserve unity and peace on shipboard amongst all passengers; and suffer no . . . offence to be given to any of the Protestants; for this end cause all acts of the Roman Catholic religion to be done as privately as may be." He also instructed the governor "to treat all Protestants with as much mildness and favor as justice would permit," and this rule was to be observed "at land as well as at sea."

In 1633 the *Ark* and the *Dove* brought over

the first band of 300 colonists to Maryland. They cruised along the shore, "to make choice of a place" that was "probable to be healthfull and fruitfull"; a place that might be easily fortified and "convenient for trade both with the English and savages." Such a spot was found, and the first settlement made near the mouth of the Potomac River. St. Mary's was the name given to it. Here, by friendliness with the Indians, gentle toleration in religious matters, and the coming in of industrious, thrifty settlers, the colony began happily.

From 1642 to 1660, while they were having religious troubles in England, and the Puritans held the chief powers, the colonists in Maryland had similar strifes between the Protestants and Catholics, and the Marylanders and Virginians. After Charles the Second came to the throne, in 1660, affairs went smoothly again in Maryland. Toleration and good laws made it once more a happy haven for people from England and from the other colonies. In 1688, at the time of the "Glorious Revolution," which put William and Mary on the English throne where James the Second had ruled so badly, there was a little rebellion in Maryland which the proprietor could not seem to settle.

Three years later, William and Mary took the

government out of Lord Baltimore's hands, making Maryland, for a time, a royal province. The land was left still in the hands of the Baltimore family, and from it they derived a large income. Both hopes of the founder had been realized. He had founded a colony where Roman Catholics had toleration and freedom of worship, and had developed a source of income for his family from his lands.

With Virginia the relations of Maryland had never been very friendly, for Virginia claimed this land to the north, and felt that Charles the First had no right to give it to his friend, Baltimore.

THE CAROLINAS, 1663.

In 1663 Virginia was troubled again by having the land to the south given to several favorites of King Charles the Second. You remember that the early English colonies sent out by Raleigh had begun their ill-fated settlements on the coast of what is now North Carolina, and the French had made an unsuccessful attempt at Port Royal in South Carolina, before the Virginia colonists came to Jamestown.

After Virginia was well established, the colonists often explored the region of North and South Carolina, considering it a part of their territory.

Here and there a few small settlements, of which they took little notice, were unknown to the king and entirely overlooked, when King Charles II. gave the whole region to five men in 1665. They at once made attempts to sell the land to settlers, offering inducements to those who would emigrate from England and other countries.

The government provided officers with high-sounding names and allowed great privileges to owners of large estates. This elaborate scheme of government was never fully carried into effect. Charleston became the chief settlement, and by 1682 had three thousand inhabitants under a good local government. Some of the colonists were French Huguenots, some Scotch Presbyterians; all were willing to work hard to build up the town. The whole colony, however, was troubled by the Spanish in Florida, who often led the Indians against them. The governors sent out by the proprietors were not always good men. They sometimes made serious trouble.

By 1688 the colony was still weak and turbulent; but the people of Charleston, by industry and trade with the other colonies, built up their city. In the later history of the colonies it took an important place.

CHAPTER XIII.

HOW THE PILGRIMS CAME TO NEW PLYMOUTH.

Do you ask why these people are gathered on this shore, some crying, others looking sadly and steadily over the ocean? Can you see away off on the horizon the sails of a ship? Find the rude log house up on the hill behind the people. Look at their faces and their clothes, then read their story; for they are the Pilgrims at Plymouth, watching their ship, the *Mayflower*, start for England, which was once their home.

It is the spring of 1621. These people have already begun the first permanent settlement on the mainland of New England. Notice the boy standing beside the old, gray-haired man, and the little girls among the women who are kneeling on the ground. Then, do you see the woman hiding her face on her husband's shoulder to conceal the tears she could not keep back? Perhaps she was trying to shut out the last glimpse of the disappearing ship which the others seem so eager to watch. Their hearts and thoughts seem to go back to England, their old home. The little children,

Departure of the "Mayflower," 1621.

however, have no remembrance of Old England, for they were not born there, nor here in New England. The only home they knew was in Holland until the *Mayflower* brought them to this new coast a few months ago.

When the ship was out of sight, the Pilgrims went back to their homes, which were small log-cabins. Then, many of the children, no doubt, asked their fathers and mothers to tell them once more the story of their lives in Old England, and why they had come to this new country to stay, while the *Mayflower* went back.

THE OLD HOME AT SCROOBY.

This is the story that the Pilgrim fathers must have told their children of their life in England:

It was a long time ago when we lived in the pretty country village of Scrooby, Nottinghamshire. Some of us were grown men and women before the opening of this seventeenth century, and the coming of Jamie, the Scotsman, to the throne so long held by his mother's enemy, Queen Elizabeth.

The century was only a few years old when we formed our church at Scrooby Manor, where Mr. William Bradford kept a post-house. We formed our church, with Mr. Bradford as ruling elder,

For our minister we called Mr. John Robinson, a learned and high-minded young man, who had studied at the University of Cambridge. We were like a great many Englishmen of that day, who were not satisfied with the Church of England. We were all called Puritans, because we thought that the beliefs of the church should be purer and the services simpler. You could not understand just what changes we wanted if you were told, so you may simply remember that we wanted to worship in what we believed to be a better way than that of the Established Church.

SEPARATISTS.

A large number of the people who wanted these changes remained in the Church, hoping to make the changes gradually. But we were of the party who believed that it was best to form a church of our own. Those who did that were called Separatists. We formed a Separatist church at Scrooby, and many people met with us from other towns near by, in Nottinghamshire and Lincolnshire. We, and all those who formed Separatist churches, drew down the ill will of James I., the archbishops, the bishops, and all the clergy and people who believed that the Established Church was right, just as it was. No Englishman, woman, or child, they said, should be allowed to hold ideas of their own about the worship of God, much less to form churches of their own.

PERSECUTION AND REFUGE IN HOLLAND.
1607-1620.

King James I. was determined, he said, "to make the Puritans conform or to harry them out of the land." When he raised Bancroft to the high office of archbishop of Canterbury, the harrying was done so thoroughly that almost all we Separatists in England fled to Holland for our lives.

The States-General, as the government of Holland was called, had lately made laws to protect everyone in their country in his own form of worship. Holland, or the Netherlands, as it was also called, was the only country in the world at that time where people could have what was termed religious liberty.

A SHORT STAY IN AMSTERDAM.

Many Separatist churches went from England to Amsterdam before we made up our minds to leave Scrooby; but the time came for us to go, too, in 1608. It was sad to leave our country homes, and the farms where our fathers and grandfathers had lived before us, and where we had hoped our children and grandchildren would live after us. Few Englishmen like foreigners. It was hard to go to a strange country where people spoke the Dutch language, which we did not understand; but when we thought of our beliefs and our church, we were all willing to face anything in order to worship God as we believed we ought to do. Elder William Brewster had traveled and lived in the Low Countries—another name for Holland. We were all willing to follow him and Mr. Robinson wherever they thought best to go. So we followed the other Separatist churches to Amsterdam. But Amsterdam is a large city. It seemed too crowded for such country-loving people as we were. Besides, the Separatist churches there were disputing among themselves, and doing a number of things that our high-minded pastor did not wish to see us do.

LEYDEN.

So, after a year, we moved to the smaller city of Leyden, where there was a great university, and where we met many good people from all parts of Europe. Captain Myles Standish, an English soldier, was one who became our stanch friend, although he never joined our church. In Leyden we all learned some trade, for we were all poor, although most of us had left comfortable homes in England. We tried to keep to our English ways, but all were obliged to learn the Dutch language for our business. Our children heard more of it than of their own. They played with Dutch children, although we did not always desire to have them. Some of our older boys and girls fell in love with young people of the Netherlands and married them, much against our wishes. Worse than all else, we found that we could earn so little money at our new trades that we must keep our children away from their play, and the fresh air, in order to make them work, to provide the clothing we needed, and food enough to keep us all alive.

NEWS OF THE NEW WORLD.

We heard how the Spaniards had opened up South America, and we wondered sometimes if we could make a home for our children there. But the Spaniards' country was a Roman Catholic country. We could not go there. Our objections to the Church of England were, that it was growing too much like the Church of Rome, from which it was separated in the time of Queen Elizabeth's father, Henry VIII.

After a time we heard that a colony had planted Jamestown, in Virginia. Again, news came that

our own countryman, Henry Hudson, had taken
possession of a beautiful country in North America, near Virginia, for the States-General of Holland. All this was talked over by Mr. Robinson,
Elder Brewster, Deacon Carver, and other members of our church. There were about three hundred of us then. At last it was decided that the
younger and stronger members of our church
should go to the New Netherland, or to Virginia.
They were to go as pioneers for the rest. Then
there was a hard time to get the permission, and
the help we needed to begin the first settlement.
The States-General refused to protect us and our
religion in America. Then, our only hope was
to find some help in England among the Puritans
in the church. Several of them were powerful
members of the Virginia Company. All Englishmen wanted colonies to settle on their claims
in America, and many thought that a little company of Separatists could do no harm in that vast
wilderness. So, at last, James I. said that if we
planted there, no one should molest us on account
of our religion.

THE MERCHANT-PARTNERS.

A merchant, by the name of Peirce, obtained
papers, called patents, from the Virginia Company

giving us permission to settle on some of their land. Peirce helped us to form a partnership with some "Merchant-Adventurers" of London, who lent us money enough for our pioneers' voyage, and to begin a settlement. Most of the merchants had no sympathy with our religion; but they thought we were so deeply in earnest that we should succeed, and pay a good interest on their loan. About one hundred of us agreed to go on the first voyage. In a solemn ceremony the Leyden church formed us into a sort of daughter church, with Elder Brewster at our head, until we should be reunited under Mr. Robinson. Our church and colony were one. We formed a colonizing company, with Deacon Carver as our governor or president, and in the name of this company we bound ourselves to the Merchant-Adventurers for seven years, until our debt to them should be paid. After seven years the property of our settlement will be divided. The Merchant-Adventurers will receive their loan and their share of our profits. Then all our property here, and our share of the profits will be divided amongst the members of the colonizing company. Meantime, we colonists agreed to have everything in common. We hope to be more successful than the colonists were in Virginia.

LEAVING LEYDEN.

It was even sadder to leave Leyden than it had been to leave England; but all were brave. Mr. Bradford said that we were Pilgrims going to the promised land at the call of God.

We sailed from the Dutch port of Delft Haven, where many of our friends from Leyden saw us off. Our boat was a small, old vessel, called the *Speedwell*. The *Mayflower*, a larger and better craft, we found at Southampton, England, waiting to join us, with a small store of provisions and tools and other things we should need in the New World. A number of our Separatist friends and some strangers, sent by the Merchant-Adventurers to work under our directions, were waiting for us in the *Mayflower*. After another sad parting, we started. In a few days the *Speedwell* sprung a leak. We put back to the port of Plymouth, moved everything possible to the *Mayflower*, and started again, leaving a number of our dearest friends behind, because there was not room for them in the *Mayflower*.

THE VOYAGE TO NEW ENGLAND.

When we started again there were one hundred and two of us, men, women, and children. A voyage of over sixty days brought us to land, but not in the region for which we had our patent. In bleak, cold, stormy weather, of early winter, the *Mayflower* came to land far north of Virginia, in the region called New England and owned by a company, who were rivals of the Virginia company, and bitterly opposed to all Puritans, especially Separatists.

It was too near winter to go farther. We came to land near Cape Cod. Some of us thought that Captain Jones was bribed to come here by the men whom the Merchant-Adventurers sent with us, because they did not like our strict ways and they thought that if we landed where we had no patent they could refuse to obey our directions. They were mostly laborers whose work was much needed. They were to dig and haul wood for us and to pay their passage in that way.

"THE MAYFLOWER COMPACT."

Elder Bradford, Governor Carver and Captain Standish knew how to deal with them. As soon as we reached the New World, but before we so much as looked for a place to settle, the wise fathers of our colony drew up what was called a compact, and all the men or "heads of families" were asked to sign it at once if they wished to have any voice in the government of the colony. Each signer bound himself to obey the laws and orders made by the whole body of the signers. Those who did not sign must obey the signers or leave the colony. There were forty-one signers, the rest of our company which numbered one hundred and two, you remember, were the Merchants' laborers,

Elder Brewster's Chair.   A Pilgrim Cradle.

a few of the Pilgrims' men and maid servants and the women, the boys and the girls of the Pilgrim families."

*   *   *   *   *

THE MAYFLOWER BABY.

The children knew the story of their life in the New World, although, perhaps, they did not know the meaning of much that took place. One event they felt was especially for their delight. Before they landed Mr. and Mrs. White had a boy-baby born to them. They called him Peregrine, which means a wanderer.

BRADFORD'S JOURNAL.

Fortunately the good Pilgrim and gifted writer, William Bradford, set down all the interesting and important events of the journey and settlement in a book, which has been in careful hands ever since. Probably the Pilgrim children were not allowed to read Mr. Bradford's manuscript; but the readers of this book may see what he wrote. It has been copied in many grown folks' histories; but now, if you go to Boston, you may see the valuable old book itself, for we have recently got it back from England, where it had been for many years.

ON CAPE COD.

The first landing was on Cape Cod. Some of the company went ashore every day, with the exception of the Sabbath. The women washed the clothes; the children were told to run and play, and stretch the young limbs that had been cramped on their long voyage. At the same time other men got out a small boat, called a shallop, which the *Mayflower* had brought over, carefully stowed between her decks. The shallop had a sail, as well as oars, and was large enough to seat twenty men. It was needed to cruise the bay beyond the cape, in search of a good harbor and place for the settle-

THE "MAYFLOWER" AND THE SHALLOP.

ment, and it was made ready for use as soon as possible. Those who were not at work on the shallop began to make

EXCURSIONS ON THE CAPE.

"Bradford's Journal" says, that on November 15th some men "were set ashore, and when they had ordered themselves in the order of a single file, and marched about the space of a mile by the sea, they espied five or six people, with a dog, coming towards them, who were savages; who, when they saw them, ran into the wood, and whistled the dog after them. . . . When the Indians saw our men following them, they ran away with might and main: and our men followed them that night about ten miles, by the trace of their footings. . . . At length night came upon them, and they were constrained to take up their lodging. So they set forth three sentinels; and of the rest, some kindled a fire, others fetched wood, and there held our rendezvous that night.

"In the morning, so soon as we could see the trace, we proceeded on our journey. We marched through boughs and bushes, and under hills and valleys, which tore our very armor in pieces, and yet could meet with none of them, nor their houses, nor find any fresh water, which we greatly desired and stood in need of; for we brought neither beer nor water with us, and our victuals was only biscuit and Holland cheese, and a little bottle of aquavitæ; so we were sore athirst. About ten o'clock we came into a deep valley, full of brush, . . . and long grass, through which we found little paths or tracks; there we saw a deer and found springs of fresh water, of which we were heartily glad, and set us down and drunk our first New England water.

A FARMING COUNTRY.

"From thence we went on, and found much plain ground, about fifty acres fit for the plough, and some signs where the Indians had formerly planted their corn. . . . We found a little path to certain heaps of sand, one whereof was covered with old mats, and had a wooden thing, like a mortar, on top of it, and an earthen pot, laid in a little hole, at the end thereof. We, musing what it might be, digged, and found a bow and, as we thought, arrows; but they were rotten. We supposed there were many other things; but, because we deemed them graves, we put in the bow again, and made it up as it was before, and left the rest untouched. . . .

"We went on further and found new stubble, of which they had gotten corn this year, and many walnut trees full of nuts. . . . Passing thus a field or two, we came to another, which had also been new gotten, and there we found where a house had been and four or five old planks laid together. Also we found a great kettle which had been some ship's kettle, and brought out of Europe. There was also a heap of sand, made like the former, but it was newly done; we might see how they had paddled it with their hands. . . . In it we found a little old basket full of fair Indian corn and digged further, and found a fine, great new basket full of very fair corn of this year, some yellow, some red, and others mixed with blue, which was a very goodly sight. The basket was round and narrow at the top. It held about three or four bushels, which was as much as two of us could lift up from the ground, and was very handsomely and cunningly made. . . . We were in suspense what to do with it and the kettle; and at length, after much consultation, we concluded to take the kettle and as much of the corn as we could carry away with us; and when our shallop came, if we could find any of the people and come to parley with them, we could give them the kettle again and satisfy them for the corn.

"So we took all the ears and put a good deal of the loose corn in the kettle for two men to bring away on a staff. Besides, they that could put any into their pockets, filled the same. . . . And thus we came, both weary and welcome, home, and delivered in our corn into the store to be kept for seed. . . . This was our first discovery whilst our shallop was in repairing."

CHAPTER XIV.

THE PLYMOUTH PLANTATION.
1620.

This is the name of Mr. Bradford's book and of the Pilgrims' colony, in what is now part of Massachusetts, for the first settlement was made, not on

Cape Cod, but on the main coast of Massachusetts Bay. There Captain John Smith had found a harbor and put it on his map of New England about six years before; and Prince Charles had named it for Plymouth, England, the same port from which the Pilgrims last sailed, you remember.

The Pilgrims reached this harbor of New Plymouth in December. An exploring party in the shallop was caught by a blinding snowstorm. The cold was so intense that the spray of the salt water froze on the men's clothing until it was like coat-of-mail, they said.

On a Friday evening, this small band of pioneers

reached the island at the entrance to the harbor. They named it after the *Mayflower's* mate, Clarke's Island. There they stayed over Sunday. Monday they sailed about the harbor. Then they landed, December 20, 1620—a date now called in New England Forefather's Day. They found brooks of fresh water, good hills for look-outs, and a large space cleared of the forest. So they decided that it would be better to make the settlement there than to spend more time in looking for a better place.

The next day they went back to the big ship to report. Three days later, the *Mayflower* weighed anchor, sailed across the southerly end of Massachusetts Bay and anchored in Plymouth Harbor.

BEGINNING WORK.

Then busy days began for all the men. They built a sort of platform on the high hill overlooking the shore. On this they planted their guns to defend the whole town. This town they soon laid out. A long street ran from the foot of the hill to the platform, with house lots on each side. Nearly every morning in the severe winter weather the men went ashore; some to cut and haul trees, some to shovel snow away from the ground where the first building was begun. This was a large log cabin for a common store-house. "Tuesday, the 9th of January, was a reasonably fair day, and we went to labor that day in the building of our town in two rows of houses, for more safety. We divided by lot the plot of ground whereon to build our town. . . . We agreed that every man

THE OLD FORT, USED ALSO AS THEIR MEETING-HOUSE.

should build his own house, thinking that by this course men would make more haste than working in common. The common house in which, for the first, we made our rendezvous, being near finished, wanted only covering." It was "about twenty foot square." It was decided that "some of us should make mortar and some gather thatch; so that in four days half of it was thatched. Frost and foul weather hindered us much. This time of the year seldom could we work half the week."

All the men seemed ready to work, and Governor Carver did not have much difficulty in keeping them to the promises made in the compact on board the *Mayflower*.

CAPTAIN MYLES STANDISH.

On Saturday, the 17th of January, in the morning, a meeting of the signers was held to establish military orders. They chose for their captain, their soldier-friend, Myles Standish, a man famous for his small figure and his great courage and military ability. From the beginning, Captain Standish was a leader in all the colony's undertakings. He was their commander and chief counsellor in their relations with the Indians and in all their military affairs.

FRIENDLY INDIANS—SAMOSET.

The colonists did not see an Indian near enough to Plymouth to speak to him until March. Several times natives were seen and heard in the distance. Often the settlers were prepared for an attack, but none was made. One day in March the newcomers were surprised by an Indian who came into the settlement alone, with words of friendly welcome in English. This was Samoset, an Indian who had learned some phrases from English fishermen on the coast, farther east, where, the Pilgrims learned, there was a large fishing trade along the coast of Maine.

The colonists returned Samoset's kindly greeting, and made him welcome to their settlement as he had made them welcome to the country. He told them many things about the natives and the place they had chosen. He said that there was no one to dispute their claim to it. The tribes who had once owned the region had died of a plague or fever a few years before.

MASSASOIT OF THE WAMPANOAGS.

After a few days Samoset made a second visit to the settlement, bringing with him five other natives. These were of the Wampanoag or Pocanoket nation. They brought presents from their chief, Massasoit, who soon came himself. Mr. Winslow and a few other Pilgrims went out to meet him on a hill near the plantation. They made him presents and proved to him that they wished to be good friends. Massasoit at that time was troubled by the Narragansett Indians, who lived to the north and west of Plymouth across the Narragansett Bay; he thought that the English were a wonderful and very powerful people, and he wanted their friendship as much as the Pilgrims wanted his. So they made a treaty which was kept by both parties to it for many, many years. It was broken long after Massasoit's death by his warlike son, whom the English called King Philip.

SQUANTO.

Another of the Pilgrims' valuable Indian friends was Squanto. He spoke more English than Samoset. He had been carried off to England years before by one of Captain John Smith's men, and had been brought back by Captain Dermer, not very long before the Pilgrims arrived. He showed the strangers the best ponds for fresh-water fish, the best places on the coast for salt-water fish. He taught them how to dig clams, which for years were often their only food. Squanto also helped in the first plantings. He taught the Englishmen how to plant the maize or Indian corn, as they called it, in rows of little hills. He told them that the ground would not be rich enough to grow the corn unless they buried a fish, called the alewife, in each little hill with the few kernels of seed. Every spring thousands of the alewives came up the creek at Plymouth from the sea.

March 6, Bradford wrote: "This day some garden seeds were sown."

SICKNESS, HUNGER AND DEATH.

The Pilgrims had much sickness and hunger, besides all they suffered from the intense cold and long storms. Half of them died before the settlement was ready to live in. The others often lacked enough to eat for weeks together.

Among those who died before the first summer came, was Governor Carver. His friends buried him sadly, upon the hill above the settlement, and leveled his grave as they did all the others, so that the Indians should not know how small the colony had grown.

THE SECOND COMPANY OF PILGRIMS, 1621.

In the *Fortune* and the *Charity* a second company of Pilgrims arrived at New Plymouth in 1621. Some of them were the friends who had been obliged to stay behind because of the *Speedwell's* leak. Others came directly from Leyden. Still others were from the Merchant-Adventurers, and were neither friends nor Separatists. One of these was a ship-carpenter, another was a skilful salt-maker, both much needed by the colony. Two others were less welcome, these were John Oldham, a trader, and John Lyford, a minister. Both of these newcomers were so disagreeable to the colonists, and made so much trouble by sending false accounts to England, that they were finally sent out of the settlement in disgrace.

THE END OF THE COMMON STORE SYSTEM.

After a year or two the Pilgrim leaders saw that the common store system did not encourage people enough to keep up their courage in their hard pioneer life. In a town meeting it was decided to allot an acre of land to every freeman, or voting man of the colony, and that he and his family be allowed certain time to work it for his own profit. The people took so much interest and pride in their own plots that the colony began to prosper as it had not done before. Still, all had a very hard time.

CO-PARTNERSHIP NOTICE, 1627.

Have you ever seen these words in a newspaper? Do you know that they mean that men who have been known as a firm or company doing business together wish to notify the public that the partnership is to come to an end? Such a time came for the Pilgrims and the Merchant-Adventurers, and we will call it by its proper name. You remember that the partnership was formed in 1620, for a term of seven years. So in 1627 the time came for a co-partnership notice.

You know what a hard time the settlers had had. By 1627 they had not succeeded enough to repay what the merchants had loaned them. Much less were there any profits to divide; but the partnership was not a pleasant one to the colonists, and a few of the leaders agreed to take the debt on their shoulders, if the merchants would release them. It was necessary for Captain Standish and Mr. Winslow and others of the most businesslike men in the colony, to go to England to arrange the matter; but finally the affair was settled. They formed an enterprising trading company, which made the Pilgrims pioneers in New England trade, as in many other things. They paid their heavy debt to the London merchants by their hard work and enterprise in fishing, and in a trade, especially for furs, among the Indians from the Connecticut River to the Kennebec. After a few years more the colonists paid those who had assumed the Merchant-Adventurers' debt, and then the colony of New Plymouth became a small, self-governing state of English freemen, with farms of their own; and every family was free to use its own judgment about its work. The settlement prospered. Meantime the colony grew. Nearly all the members of the church in Leyden came over, although Mr. Robinson died before the main body started. In 1630 there were three hundred people in the settlement. In 1643 three thousand were living comfortably in eight small towns, grouped about the first plantation, which was finally called Plymouth, while the colony was always New Plymouth.

By that time the pioneer days were over. The larger Puritan colony, which settled about Massachusetts Bay, making Boston their capital, proved more attractive than the old colony in many ways.

The Pilgrims in Plymouth did their great work in the early years. When they came to New England, "the discoverer, the gold-seeker, the merchant, had all attempted the task of colonization, with varying success. Now, for the first time, religious enthusiasts attempted it." You have learned about their success. They had realized from the beginning what one of their leaders said before this band of pioneers left Holland for the New World, that "all great and honorable actions are accompanied with great difficulties, and must be both enterprised (or undertaken) and overcome with answerable courages."

In 1691 King William and Queen Mary of England annexed the "Old Colony" to "the Bay," and placed Massachusetts under the government of a royal province.

CHAPTER XV.

THE COLONY OF MASSACHUSETTS BAY.

"By a colony we mean a societie of men, drawn out of one state . . . and transplanted into another country." So wrote an Englishman, in 1630.

That year just such a "societie," or body of men, women and children, were drawn, by their own desires and longings, out of England into America. We know them by the name of the place where they settled, the Massachusetts Bay Colony. They made many settlements on the shores of this bay and the rivers flowing into it. To know why they came we must go back to the story of

THE PURITANS IN THE CHURCH OF ENGLAND.

You remember that they did not want to separate from the national church, as the Pilgrims did, but to change the service to simpler forms. They stayed in the church, with some change, and became very strong toward the close of the first quarter of the seventeenth century. They became so strong that the churchmen who believed in the old forms decided that their power must be broken once for all.

James I. died about this time, and his son took the throne, as Charles I. Charles made Archbishop Laud his favorite, and raised into power new men, who promptly turned the church into what the Puritans called its " march backward." Besides that, Laud and his party made it their business to put the Puritans out of favor at court, too, and drove them from all the high public offices.

The next step was to find some excuse to deprive them of their titles and estates.

A REFUGE IN NEW ENGLAND

The Puritans said among themselves: We cannot do better than to leave the country while we may, and let us found a colony of our own in New England, where we can have such church services and government as we think Englishmen ought to have. This plan interested many rich and powerful men and women of the great English families. They were quiet about it, for fear Charles I. and Laud should hear of it, and put an end to it. But they worked rapidly. They formed a company for trade and fishing, and secured a grant from the Council for New England to certain right to trade and make settlements within a region of about sixty miles inland from the shore of the Massachusetts Bay, from three miles north of the Merrimac to three miles south of the Charles. The king gave the company his royal charter, supposing it was merely a company to improve English trade in America, and to build factories, such as the Dutch had set up on the Hudson, the Connecticut, and the Delaware. His majesty had no idea that he was chartering a Puritan commonwealth in New England. Yet, as soon as his parchments passed the Great Seal of England, the Puritans began to slip away from England to plant a dozen towns on the Bay, and by and by they set up their charter government over what was almost an independent state, with Boston for their capital.

THE PIONEERS AT SALEM, 1628.

The Van, or pioneers of the Bay Company's settlers, were sent out under Mr. John Endicott, to "provide against the wants of a Desart Wilderness." They went to a place called Naumkeag. Some fishermen, from Dorchester, England, were waiting for them under a man named Roger Conant, who made peace in more than one quarrel. One of these quarrels was between the Dorchester men and Endicott's party. When it was settled they decided to call the place Salem, which is a Bible word for peace.

"SERVANTS" OF THE COMPANY.

Many of Endicott's colony were servants of the Puritans who formed the Bay Company, much as many of the Jamestown settlers had been under bondage to the London Company of Virginia. "Those that were sent over as servants, having itching desires after novelties, found a readier way to make an end of their masters' provisions than they could find means to get more. They that came over their own men [at their own cost], had but little left to feed on, and most began to repent. . . . for they had but little corne," so that "they were forced to lengthen out their owne food with acorns."

THE SALEM CHURCH.

Another party was sent out to Salem as soon as possible with two ministers.

The Puritans of the new colony wished to form some such church as they had hoped to make of the Church of England. They had no wish to be Separatists like the Plymouth Pilgrims. Indeed, they were very indignant if any one classed them with the Separatists. They simply desired a purer form of the Church of England.

Perhaps they had a clearer idea of what they did not want than of what they did want. After all, circumstances seemed to shape the forms of worship which they established here. There were no large churches, with stained-glass windows, nor statues in the chancel for any one to find fault with; no organs or surpliced choirs for them to question. Neither was there a bishop to consecrate their churches and decide upon their ministers. They had not determined how they would form their churches, when they were told of the simple, happy, pure church at New Plymouth. It was Separatist, to be sure, but it was a good church, and the Salem people soon decided that they could not do better than to form another on the same plan.

"As soon as the ministers landed, Mr. Higginson and Mr. Skelton were elected to the office of pastor and teacher, respectively. Each, then, in turn, ordained the other by laying hands on him." Then a church covenant, or system of faith and discipline, was drawn up by Higginson, and accepted by thirty of the settlers." This is the account of the beginning of the little church at Salem, started by the Van, as we call them.

GROWTH OF THE COLONY, 1630-1640.

Eighty people died that winter in the settlement, partly on account of the scarcity of food. It was a hard season for the pioneers. One of them says, in the old-fashioned spelling of that time: "Yet some delighting their eye with the rarity of things present and feeding their fancies with new discoveries at the spring's approach, they made shift to rub out the winter's cold by the fireside having fuell enough growing at their very doores. . . . discoursing between one while and another of the great progress they would make after the summer sun had changed the earth's white furr'd gowne into a greene mantell."

When this green mantle was in full view more ships came from England, bringing to Massachusetts Bay the first large body of pioneers, under John Winthrop, the Governor of the colony. They were surprised to find their pioneers at Salem in such a miserable plight, with neither homes for themselves nor for the newcomers. To add to their trouble, the ships loaded with provisions did not arrive until long after they were expected, the common store of food was so nearly gone that, in order to keep from starving, they were obliged to set free one hundred and eighty servants "to shift for themselves."

THE COMPANY'S GOVERNMENT.

In England, meantime, many people joined the company; that is, they paid money to be used by the company, and received shares in the company's rights. Some hoped to gain profit from the trade and fisheries, but more desired merely to join the colony. They were called the freemen of the company; now they would be known as stockholders. The whole body of these freemen were to meet in the "great and general court" (what we should call a stock-holders' annual meeting) once a year to elect a governor, deputy-governor and several councillors, who were called a board of assistants (about the same as directors of a company). At the general courts the freemen also made by-laws to govern the company in any way that they saw fit if it did not conflict with the laws of England—just as railroad companies now make by-laws for their roads. Once in three months quarter courts or quarter sessions were held by the freemen. The governors and assistants met once a month.

If you think a moment you will see that this
company, with its freemen, its courts and its governor
and assistants had all the responsibility for
the colony. But a colony is not like a railroad;
for it must have laws and government; and most
of the stockholders or freemen were now in America,
and could not attend meetings in England.
So the Puritan members thought it best quietly to
move the company, charter and all, to their colony.
All the points of law were looked up—they thought
it could be done without losing any rights or privileges.
The governor, Matthew Craddock, decided
to remain in England as the company's agent,
and the other officers in London were kept the
same as usual. John Winthrop was elected as the
new governor, to go to the colony, and the whole
action was carried out before Laud or the king
knew a word about it.

"THE GREAT EMIGRATION."
1630.

Hundreds of families in England secretly spent
the winter of 1630 in preparing to go to Massachusetts
Bay. Dozens of pairs of shoes of various
sizes were ordered. Dozens of hats, of swords, of
bed and bolster ticks, were bargained for. The
orders were distributed among the different makers
and tradesmen of the large cities, so that suspi-

cions should not be aroused. Toward spring provisions were gathered—cheese, sugar, salted and smoked meats, and many other things. Then seeds, tools and fishing-tackle.

In April the Great Emigration began with the sailing of the governor and assistants, and several hundred people, in four good ships, the *Arabella*, *Jewell*, *Ambrose* and *Talbot*.

The voyage was a hard one, of nearly four months. Mists and heavy winds delayed and endangered the ships, yet all reached the Salem harbor in safety. You have already heard of the condition of affairs at Salem. Perhaps it was just as well that houses had not been built for all the new settlers there, for the new comers decided that the place did not please them. Some went further south and settled what they called Charlton, or Charlestown, on a hilly point near the mouth of the Charles River, also named for that very King Charles, from whom they had taken such care to slip away. Others made the settlement of Meadford, now Medford, on the Mystick River. Others built Watertown, "Rocksbury," Dorchester, and Newtown, which was named Cambridge after a few years, when a college was opened there. But very soon the largest town in the colony was Boston, of which we shall read further on.

THE INDEPENDENT CHURCH OF NEW ENGLAND.

Almost all of these towns were founded by congregations from England, who kept together with their ministers, and who soon set up their churches as the Salem people had done, on the plan of the Pilgrims' church at New Plymouth. They were called the Independent, and afterward the Congregational, Churches of New England. The "sin of separation" from the Church of England seemed less terrible after they came across the ocean and found how much they had in common with the Separatists. While they borrowed much of the church discipline and form of government from Plymouth, the mass of the people did not accept its mildness or toleration. Soon no churches were allowed in Massachusetts except on this Congregational model.

THE FIRST CHURCH.

Religion of a severe sort entered into all the duties and pleasures of the Bay colonists' lives. It controlled their political affairs also; for here, the churches and towns were controlled by the same men. Those who were not church members were soon left out of a share in the government, for freemen of the company voted that to have a vote in the Massachusetts Bay Colony, or to hold office, a man must belong to the church in his town. Services and doctrines were alike in all the towns, and hence all those who had a part in public affairs were expected to have the same religious beliefs. You know that the Puritans left England and faced all these hardships to make a place to live where they, and the people who believed as they did, might worship unharmed.

Perhaps you have heard the story of the king, who, having spent much of his life in making all his people believe alike, retired to a quiet monastery. Then, for pastime, he tried to regulate the clocks. He never succeeded in making all of them tick alike. Then he began to wonder if it was any more possible to make all people think and believe alike.

The Puritans of the Massachusetts settlements did not insist that every one must believe just as they did; but they said that any one who did not agree with the majority could not vote; and any one who made his difference of opinion too public, could not live in the colony. This was why Roger Williams was sent away, and later the Quakers were persecuted for persisting in their peculiar religious beliefs.

EARLIER SETTLERS ON THE BAY.

The Puritans found several small plantations of farmers and fishermen about Massachusetts Bay. All of them had been made since the plantation at New Plymouth. One was at Weymouth, one at Nantasket, another at Mt. Wollaston. On Noddles Island, now East Boston, they found Mr. Samuel Maverick, "a man of very loving and courteous behaviour, very ready to entertain strangers."

SHAWMUT, WHERE BOSTON WAS BUILT.

Another good man, named John Blackstone, and called "Blaxton," had a farm on the most attractive and central of all the places in the bay, a peninsula made up of three hills, and almost surrounded by water.

BLACKSTONE'S HOUSE.

The Indians called this peninsula Shawmut, because it had springs of good water. When some of the colony settled Charlestown, opposite, they called this attractive place the Trimountain, or Tramount, for its three hills.

At first Newtown was chosen for the fortified capital of the colony, but the governor and assistants soon saw that their main seaport, their stronghold, and the seat of their government, should be on the harbors and hills of the Tramount peninsula, in the centre of the semicircle of settlements on the bay. The Company bought the land of Mr. Blaxton, and of the Indians. Governor Winthrop removed his house from Newtown, and at a General Court, held September 7, 1630, the town was named Boston. Many of the leaders in the colony were from Boston, in Lincolnshire, England. To make the name doubly dear to them, Mr. Cotton, their favorite minister in Boston, England, came three years later to live and preach in Boston, New England.

THE THREE HILLS.

All the towns were called upon to help build a fort at Boston, where all might have protection in case of an attack from enemies. A stockade was built on what was then called Fort Hill. A beacon, to call people from the neighboring towns in case of danger, gave the name to Beacon Hill. The beacon was a tar-barrel on the end of a tall

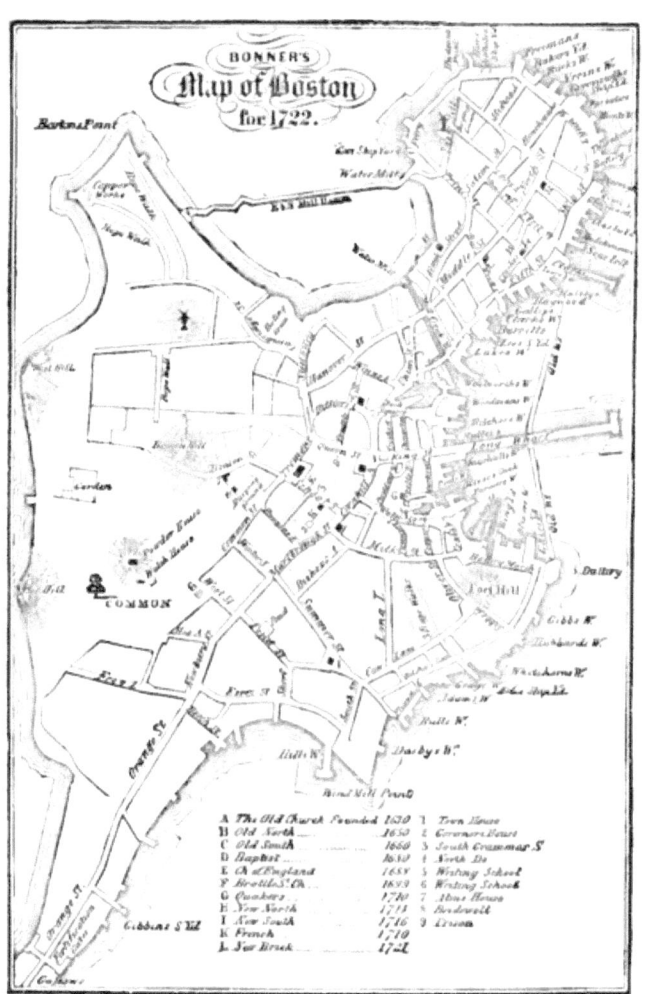

pole; when the barrel was set on fire, all the men, far and near, knew that they must leave their own affairs to defend their new country. Usually a man on horseback galloped through one village after another to tell the people what was the danger, and what the authorities in Boston demanded of them. The third hill was called Snow Hill.

Boston is now a large city; but it still has the names of some of its hills, besides its Tremont Street, Shawmut Avenue, and many other reminders of the old times.

THE FIRST WINTER

of the great immigration to New England was a hard one. Like all new-comers, the colonists suffered from the cold and the scarcity of good food. There was much sickness and many deaths. Some were brave and unselfish; some were lazy and discontented. In the spring about one hundred of the selfish ones went back to England; "and glad were we so to be rid of them," said one of the old writers.

CHAPTER XVI.

THE COLONISTS' WRITINGS.

You may read in the people's own words why they came to Massachusetts Bay, how they fared on the long sea voyage, what awaited them, and how they lived and loved in the new country. We have their letters, pamphlets and books, which were written in the colony and sent to friends in England. Sometimes these writings were put away in the desks of the people who received them, and, years after, were found by their children, or, perhaps, by their grandchildren. The pamphlets were usually printed in some small, dingy printer's shop in Massachusetts, or far away in England. Swinging from an iron rod over the door, was a quaint sign which was mentioned in the odd title-pages, such as this one:

"The Simple Cobler of Aggawam in America."

*   *   *   *   *

Printed by J. D. & R. L. for Stephen Bowtell, at the Sign of the Bible, in Pope's Head Alley, in 1647.

The early books are so old and musty now that

you would not care to look at them, if you did not know that they contain stories about the colonies that were written by the people who helped to plant them. They are written in quaint language and spelling; for at that time people had not agreed how words should always be spelled.

ATTRACTIONS IN MASSACHUSETTS.

The colonists who were determined to stay, sent letters to their friends and old neighbors in England, urging them to come out. They named many inducements. They wrote of the fertility of the soil, the rank growth of the grass that would feed many cattle. "In our plantation," wrote a minister, "we have already a quart of milk for a penny." "Little children here, by setting of corn, may earn much more than their own maintenance."

The new vegetables and wild flowers delighted the English. About Massachusetts Bay were "plentie of single Damaske Roses verie sweet." In the rivers and bay were all kinds of fish, good to eat. The bass, the colonists said, was a new fish, "most sweet and wholesome." There was an "aboundance of lobsters, that the least boy in the plantation may both catch and eat what he will of them." There were means to make salt to keep the fish for winter use, which was most important. "Here are likewise aboundance of Turkies, often killed in the Woods, farre greater than our English Turkies and exceeding fat, sweet, and fleshy, for here they have aboundance of feeding all the yeere long as strawberries; in Summer all places are full of them and all manner of Berries and fruits."

"Our Pine-trees that are the most plentiful of all wood, doth allow us plentie of candles which are verie useful in a House, and they are such candles as the Indians commonly use, having no others. They are nothing else but the wood of the Pine-tree cloven in two little slices something (or somewhat) thin, which are so full of moysture of Turpentine and Pitch that they burn as cleere as a Torch."

Many of the colony's pioneers came with their older sons. The wives and younger children remained in England, until the new homes were ready for them. Governor Winthrop came with his sons, while Mrs. Winthrop and the younger children waited in England.

GOVERNOR WINTHROP'S LETTER TO HIS WIFE,

written at Charlestown in July, 1630, says: "I shall expect thee next sommer, . . . and by that tyme I hope to be provided for thy comfortable entertainment. Howsoever our fare be but

STATUE OF GOVERNOR JOHN WINTHROP.

coarse in respect of what we formerly had (pease puddings and fish beinge o' [our] ordinary diet) yet God makes it sweet and wholesome to us (so) that I may truely say I desire no better. . . . I see no cause to repente of o' coming hither and thou seest (by o' experience) that God can bring safe hither even the tenderest women and the youngest children. . . . Be sure to be warme clothed and to have store of fresh provisions, eggs putt up in salt . . . butter, ote meale, pease and fruits, and a large stronge chest or two, well locked, to put these provisions in, and be sure they be bestowed in the ship where they may be readyly come by. . . . Be sure to have ready at see 2: or 3: skillets of severall syzes, a large fryinge panne, a small stewinge panne, and a case to boyle a pudding in. . . . Thou must be sure to bringe no more companye than so many as shall have full provisions for a yeare and a halfe, for though the earth heere be very fertile yet there must be tyme and meanes to raise it [food], if we have corne enough we may live plentifully. The Lords will in due tyme lett us see the faces of each other again to o' great comfort. . . . I kisse and blesse you all my dear children, Forth, Mary, Deane, Sam, and the others. Let my sonne provide 12 axes of several sorts of the Braintree Smith . . . whatsoever they coste, and some augurs, great and small, and many other necessaryes, which I cant now thinke of, as candles, sope, etc. Once again farewell, my dear wife

"Thy faithful husband,

"Jo: Winthrop."

Many letters were written by other husbands to their wives and carried across the Atlantic by ship captains or by friends going "home" on business or pleasure. After a few years nearly all the pioneer families were reunited. Many had good frame or brick houses, happy and comfortable with the neighbors they had had in Old England, often with the same minister, too.

MRS. WINTHROP AND THE CHILDREN

arrived in November, 1631, in the ship *Lyon*, which brought "in all sixty persons, who all arrived in good health, and lost none of their company but two children." One of them was little Ann, the governor's year and a half old daughter, who had died on the sea-voyage. Mrs. Winthrop's landing must have been filled with both joy and sorrow: joy to see her husband and have the family united once more, but sorrow for two who were missing; for besides little Ann they had lost a grown up son, Henry, who had come out with his father. He was drowned in the harbor of Salem. The reception of the colonists must have given her pleasure. After firing guns in honor of their landing, "divers of the assistants and most of the people of the near plantations, came to welcome them, and brought and sent for divers days, great store of provisions, as fat hogs, kids, venison, poultry, geese, partridges, etc., so as the like joy and manifestation of love had never been seen in New England. It was a great marvel that so much people and such store of provisions could be gathered together at so few hours' warning."

The next day was made a day of thanksgiving. Besides his Boston house, where the governor lived most of his life, he had a country home and plantation on the Mystick River, which he called Ten-Hills, and still another, called the Garden, on Governor's Island in the harbor. The children's happiest summers, probably, were passed at the Garden.

BOSTON'S PROSPERITY.

The capital of the colony grew fast. There was work for shop-keepers and mechanics. There were fishing and ship-building, and soon the town was the centre of a lively trade. Ipswich, Salem, Charlestown, Newtown, Dorchester and other towns had good harbors, but Boston was the most important. Besides the trade between the different settlements of the colony, commerce soon began with the other colonies. Some vessels went to the Maine fisheries, and others to the New Netherlands, to Virginia, and even to the Spaniards of the West Indies.

On the fourth of July, 1631, *The Blessing of the Bay* was launched. This boat was owned by Governor Winthrop and had been built for him on the Mystick River near his plantation, Ten-Hills. It was known as the pioneer of New England commerce, for it traded in all the colonies of the coast up and down the Connecticut River, through the Long Island Sound and up the Hudson River also. Before many years, trade was carried on with the English and Spanish colonies in the Bermuda Islands and the West Indies.

The *Trial*, the first ship built at Boston, carried fish to one of the islands, got wine and sugar there, took this cargo to another island and traded for cotton and tobacco, or for old iron saved by these islanders from vessels wrecked on their coast. This iron was used for New England ships.

FISHERIES AND TRADE.

When the English merchants heard how trade had begun to grow over here, and that they could

get large quantities of salt and dried fish in the
New England ports, they were more willing to
send their vessels over with passengers. They
were sure of a good return cargo, which they could
sell in the Indies, in Spain or in England.

The early English expected to make money by
the fur trade with the Indians, as the French and
Dutch did. In that trade there were many months
of idleness for the men it was necessary to keep
at the factories or stations. The Englishmen could
waste no time. They soon began to give closer
attention to the fisheries, and before long the governor
and his assistants agreed that "commerce
beginning in furs had now established itself upon
the fisheries." Most of the sea-ports of the bay
became fishing ports. If you go now to Marblehead,
Gloucester and many old towns on the Massachusetts
coast and to some villages on the Maine
shore, you can see many things to suggest the fishing
industry of New England two centuries and a
half ago.

THE KING'S DISCOVERY.

Religion was a part of every joy and sorrow,
every ordinary and extraordinary event of the
Puritans' lives. The colonists were just beginning
to enjoy living in freedom when they heard that

Archbishop Laud had discovered what they had done. From that day on the lives of the Massachusetts Bay colonists were filled with fear that the strong arm of the Church of England would stretch across the ocean and harass them, if it did not destroy their church and charter, too.

Laud told the king, of course, what he heard that the Puritans were doing, under cover of the Massachusetts Bay Company. Charles sent at once to the London office for Governor Craddock. The answer was that there was no Governor Craddock. The governor was in New England. Mr. Craddock was merely the London business agent of the company. His majesty "found, too late, that he had eagerly pounced upon a dummy." He then issued a royal command for the return of the charter. But he had not issued the charter to be held in any one place, and the leaders of the colony had been careful to look up all the points of law concerning the transfer before they made it. So, when his majesty's orders were received, they sent back courteous but evasive answers, and kept their charter in a safe place.

In those days, if a king wished to forbid further use of privileges he had granted by charter, he called for the document, and slashed it with an official sword. So, usually, people kept their privileges so long as they could keep their charters safe and whole. Every time the order for the Bay Company's charter was repeated, these wise leaders found some excuse for delay. At length Charles I. had so many troubles at home to think of that he let the colonists alone. They grew stronger and more independent every year. When Laud's persecutions ceased, few new colonists left England. The pioneer days were over for the Massachusetts Bay Colony, but not for the people who left the bay to form new colonies.

CHAPTER XVII.

**THE SMALLER COLONIES OF NEW ENGLAND.
CONNECTICUT.**

THE first colony that left the Massachusetts Bay was founded by a new set of pioneers, who made their way overland to the Connecticut River. These colonists were part of the towns and congregations of Watertown, Dorchester and Newtown (which, you remember, was afterwards called Cambridge).

These people had been settled in Massachusetts only a few years, but they thought the government too strict and religious restrictions too narrow. In asking permission, however, to remove from Massachusetts, the Connecticut pioneers gave as their chief reason, that they needed more accommodation for their cattle than they could have in their present settlement at Newtown. They urged also that the valley of the Connecticut River was rich and fruitful; that the English colonists should settle there before the Dutch, who already had one fort there.

Mr. Hooker, the minister of Newtown, went with nearly his whole congregation through the woods to make their pioneer settlement. Picture them travelling through a strange country beyond the frontiers of Massachusetts, part of the way through forests, driving one hundred and sixty cattle for which they were searching new pasturage. These cattle added their share to the undertaking by providing milk for the wanderers. The Newtown congregation settled the town of Hartford. The Dorchester people founded Windsor. The Watertown emigrants made Weathersfield. By the close of 1636 there were eight hundred English on the Connecticut. They soon united as one colony, under a constitution which they made for themselves. Their government will always be important for two things: because it was the first written American constitution and because it was more liberal than any government Englishmen had ever known. Church membership was not made a requirement for the political privileges of the town. Only the governor need be a church member in order to hold the office. The colony prospered; the people began very early to provide their children a good education. The schools, the religious toleration combined with a firm, well-established government, attracted new settlers, and the River Colony grew until it was soon a powerful rival of the great Bay Colony.

NEW HAVEN.

The city of New Haven, which is now within the boundaries of Connecticut, was begun by a separate colony of Puritans from England. Theophilus Eaton, a merchant of London, and John Davenport, a clergyman, were anxious to leave England to find a place for purer forms of worship. They were not satisfied with Massachusetts or any of the other colonies. They landed in Boston in the autumn of 1637 and stayed there over winter. In spite of inducements of the people there, and the hesitancy of some of their own party to go into a wilder, more unsettled region, the leaders kept to their original plan of a new colony. In the spring they went down to the shores of Long Island Sound, to a place west of the mouth of the Connecticut River, where they settled New Haven.

There, as in Massachusetts, only church members could be voters. The rule in the ordering of government was the "Word of God." Mr. Davenport was the minister; Mr. Eaton was the governor for twenty years. Meanwhile similar settlements, Guilford, Milford and Stamford had grown into towns with laws like those of New Haven. They were admitted into a sort of confederacy or federal government of which New Haven was chief.

Combined with the idea of a settlement where pure forms of worship might be established, was the plan of making New Haven a commercial colony. Mr. Eaton, with the instincts of a merchant, had this plan in mind when he chose a port on the Sound as the site of New Haven. Large sums were invested in ships and cargoes, but disaster after disaster, one disappointment after another, disheartened the hopes of trade and decreased the wealth of many of the merchant colonists. Then trade increased, good luck seemed to attend the vessels, and the settlement grew rich.

PROVIDENCE.

One of the greatest of the New England pioneers was Roger Williams, who founded the city of Providence and the colony of Rhode Island about the time that the towns from Massachusetts removed to Connecticut.

Do you remember that Governor Winthrop's wife and little children came over in the *Lyon* in 1631? Do you remember that there were several other passengers? Among them were Roger Williams and his wife. Roger Williams was a young man who had been educated for a clergyman and had Puritan views. In Boston he was so much respected and admired that the people wanted

him at once for the church in that town. But his
religious beliefs were not just like those of the
Puritans of Boston, so that he lost friends. Then
he went to Salem to preach; then to Plymouth.
But he soon returned to Salem. By that time
Mr. Cotton and several of the Boston leaders
were alarmed at Mr. Williams's views and his influence. There were long debates and a great trial.
Mr. Williams was warned to keep his views to
himself, but with all his friends about him, it was
impossible for him, a minister, not to talk to them.
He believed that the men of the colony should not
be shut out of the government if they were not
church members. He believed also that the King
of England had no right to give away the Indians' land. These were things that seemed
very important in those days, and Mr. Williams
was told that he must keep quiet about them or
leave the colony. He barely escaped arrest by
going out of Salem secretly in the depths of winter.
He went to the region of the Narragansett Bay.
The Indians knew him far and wide because he
was always a good friend to them and had learned
their language. Near the head of Narragansett
Bay, Williams built himself a house. His wife
and friends joined him, and the colony of Providence was established with a government which

had nothing to do with any church. People of all religions were made welcome. It was the first place in the world where there was absolute religious freedom.

PORTSMOUTH.

A few years after Williams was banished from the Massachusetts colony, others were sent out because their views differed from those of Mr. Cotton and the other leaders. Among these were Mrs. Anne Hutchinson and her followers and Mr. William Coddington who followed Mr. Williams to the Narragansett country, and settled on the north end of the island called Rhode Island.

Mr. Coddington was an energetic man, who had been quite important in Boston and was known as the man who owned the first brick house there. He seemed fitted for a leader, and the pioneer settlements he started were successful.

The land he bought from the Indian chiefs of the Narragansetts, Cannonicus and Miantinomi, for forty fathoms of white beads, which were to be equally divided between them. Coddington, in behalf of his fellow-purchasers, promised to give also " ten coates and twenty howes " to the Indian inhabitants of the island, to induce them to go away from it quietly. In the receipts of the sachems we find that twenty-three coats and thirteen hoes were given to them instead of the stipulated number; perhaps hoes were more valuable than coats to the pioneers beginning to cultivate new land.

The town of Portsmouth was laid out about a pond of fresh water. A spot was chosen for the "meeting-house," and a piece of land "to lye as a common field," for pasturage for the whole town. Then they allotted six acres to each of the freemen. One freeman was given permission to set up a house of entertainment, and given the right to brew beer, to sell " wines of strong waters " and provisions. Another freeman was allowed to set up a bakery, while a third was urged and encouraged to build a water-mill.

Like all other pioneer settlements, one of its earliest problems was how to provide for its defence. A training band was begun, made up of all men over sixteen and less than fifty years of age. Every one was summoned to train for a certain number of days in the year, or, as they said, they " were warned thereto."

Each inhabitant of the island was to be provided always with one musket, one pound of powder, twenty bullets and a sword, ready for service. They never had much trouble with the Indians, who had seemed perfectly satisfied with the price paid for the land and with a few extra gifts, wisely made. This first settlement was called Portsmouth.

NEWPORT.

In 1639 William Coddington and a part of the Portsmouth colonists went to the southwestern end of the island, to settle about a good harbor they had found there. This town, called Newport, was soon fairly started, and a trade begun with other colonies.

You will hear more of it in the period of the Revolutionary War.

Other towns grew up on the mainland round about Narragansett Bay. Later they got one common charter, as the colony of Rhode Island and Providence Plantations. All people were allowed freedom of religion there, and they should have been happy, because the government tolerated all their churches; but it was an odd, unruly colony. Each thought his own church right, and for a long time there were constant bickerings and disputes. But this trouble passed away, and a good government was established at last.

NEW HAMPSHIRE.

The colony of New Hampshire was the result of " commercial enterprise in England and religious dissensions in Massachusetts." The land was granted to John Mason in 1629; he sold it to bands of colonists, and got people to come from England to reap the benefits of trade. Others came from Massachusetts, where their religious beliefs made other people uncomfortable and themselves unwelcome. At the same time that many of Mrs. Anne Hutchinson's followers went to Rhode Island, many more went to New Hampshire. Mason spent his last years in making an elaborate scheme of government for his colony, which had so few people in it that nearly every person would have had an office if the scheme had been put in operation. In 1679 Charles II. took the colony into his own control, and made it a royal province; and, with the exception of a short interval, about the year 1688, it remained a royal province till it became an independent state. The towns, settled by people from different places, at different times, and with different aims, had few interests in common. Hence political growth was slow and slight in New Hampshire.

MAINE.

In 1638 an English traveler, John Josselyn, made a trip from Boston along the shores of Maine. He said it was "a meer wilderness," with here and there by the sea-side, a few scattered plantations, with as few houses." The man who stepped ashore must carry a gun, if he did not wish to be devoured by wolves. Gradually these shores were dotted with prosperous settlements of fishermen, while through the interior of the country fur-traders established trading-posts. The people who came to settle there were many times servants of Englishmen, who owned the lands, but did not care to live in Maine. The others were rough and poor.

In 1652 Maine became a part of Massachusetts. When the commissioners were sent over in 1665 they separated the colonies again. This, like other parts of their work, was undone as soon as their backs were turned. Massachusetts took Maine back, and it was a part of the colony and the state of Massachusetts until 1820.

CHAPTER XVIII.

THE DUTCH OF NEW NETHERLAND.
1609-1664.

The Dutch pioneers in America were led by an Englishman, Henry Hudson, who was looking for a northwest passage to China.

M-Manhattan { Where New Amsterdam was founded New York now stands.

In 1609 the Dutch East India Company sent the bold Captain Hudson in the *Half-moon* to find a northeast passage to India beyond Norway, through the Arctic Ocean. Hudson started on this voyage, but gave it up on account of the cold. He did not go back to Holland, however.

HUDSON'S SEARCH FOR A WESTERN PASSAGE TO INDIA.

He took a westward course across the Atlantic toward the countries of Virginia and New England, of which he had heard from his friend, Captain John Smith. His plan was to seek a northwest passage to India for the Dutch Company. The first land he made was Newfoundland. Then he sailed southwestward to Delaware Bay, and entered it. Next, he sailed northward, to a great harbor, from which he entered the river that now bears his name. After going up the river till it grew shallow, he recrossed the Atlantic, to tell his news in Holland. Though he knew that his great river was not the passage to China, he told the Dutch about the Indians he had seen, and he believed that they would supply a large fur-trade.

The news seemed satisfactory to the Netherland merchants who had sent Hudson. Some people think that they had given him orders to go to America; but to start as if in search of a northeast passage, so that neither Spain, France, nor England would try to stop him.

WHAT ATTRACTED THE DUTCH TO AMERICA.

The Dutch had heard of the Spanish, the French and the English trade in the New World. Naturally, they wanted some for themselves. The Netherlands had but just thrown off the yoke under which Spain had held them for many years. The treasure which the Spaniards had taken in South

America had enabled them to carry on a long war with the Netherlands. The Spaniards wanted to control the Dutch trade, and to force the Dutch people to remain in the Roman Catholic church. The Hollanders, like some of the English called Puritans, and of the French, called Huguenots, believed that people should be free to worship as they chose. At last the Dutch made a mighty effort; and by using all their wealth for seamen and ships, and by some of the noblest resistance in history, they won their freedom from Spain. When that was done, their next care was to find some good use for these brave sailors and big ships, and, at the same time, to make new fortunes in place of those spent in the long wars. By 1609 Spain had agreed to a peace; but there was no telling when it might be broken. So, to make themselves stronger, and to weaken Spain, the Dutch people determined to get a share in the New World.

With this in mind, you can imagine how pleased the Dutch people were when Hudson brought them his news. Offers were made by the government to men and companies of men who would go out to this region to start trading-posts. The Dutch have always claimed that they discovered the Hudson, and made the first settlements there; but Verrazano anchored his French *Dauphine* in the Bay long before that; and the Spaniards claim that their explorers knew the region, and had named many places on their maps before Hudson left the Netherlands.

THE ISLAND OF MANHATTAN.

Spaniards say that they gave the name of Manhattan to the island you are to hear about in this story. This long, narrow island at the mouth of the Hudson and the East Rivers was seen from the first to be important. On the early Dutch maps the name was spelt Monados, Manados, or Manatoes. Still later, Manhattoes was the spelling, then Manhattan. Some say it is an Indian name. There is a Spanish word, *monados*, which means drunken men. Perhaps some Spanish sailors landed there and made themselves intoxicated in their merrymakings after a long cruise. But the Spaniards gave little attention to the North Atlantic shore. Peter Martyr, one of their writers, showed their spirit when he said: "To the South, to the South, for the great and exceeding riches; . . . they that seek gold must not go to the cold and frozen north."

Manhattan and the Hudson had no gold for the Spanish adventurer; but the entire region of the Great River teemed with riches for the hardworking Dutch trader. Hudson saw it. Merchants of Amsterdam promptly sent men to gather it. They sent hardy traders to deal fairly with the Indians, and to build up a great trade with them as fast as possible. The country was full of natives, who would gladly barter large quantities of the skins of the otter, beaver, and other fur-bearing animals for a few beads and tin cups, or pieces of coarse red flannel. These peltries, as they were called, sold for gold in Europe.

THE FIRST DUTCH FACTORIES.

Trading-stations, called factories, were set up by the Dutch soon after Hudson returned—some people say in the next year. At first the Dutch thought that the most important place would be some distance up the Hudson. Our city of Albany was started by one of their trading-houses, built in a rough log-cabin fort. Another factory was set up on the southern end of Manhattan Island. In 1615 a solid block-house of logs was built there.

THE DUTCH WEST INDIA COMPANY, 1621.

This was chartered by the States General of Holland in 1621, to establish a colony with military government, and all rights to trade over all the region they claimed as the New Netherland. That region was from what they called the South Bay and River (now the Delaware), to what they called the Varche, or Fresh River (now the Connecticut).

The West India Company sent colonists, and promised to protect people of all Christian religions. Their first large company of settlers were some people called Walloons, who came to New Netherland from the southern part of Belgium.

These Walloons and a few Dutch colonists settled on Manhattan, and also on the two opposite shores, making the beginning of what are now Brooklyn and Jersey City. Others went up the Hudson to Fort Orange, now Albany.

THE DUTCH COMPANY'S DIRECTORS.

The governors of the colony were called directors. They were what we would call managers. They were not always good men. No one staid long. The first was Cornelius Jacobsen Mey, who has left his name on what we call Cape May, New Jersey.

The second director was Peter Minuit. By his time the company had learned the important position of Manhattan Island, and had decided that it should be the centre of the government and trade of all the New Netherland. So Minuit bought the island from the Indians for about $24, and placed a fort at one end of it. This fort was soon the centre of a settlement called New Amsterdam. Amsterdam was the name of the chief city in the home country which took a great interest in this namesake. A letter written by Peter Schagen, a citizen of Amsterdam, was sent to the Dutch government there, telling them about the growth and condition of their colony in the new world, in 1626. This is what he said:

"High and Mighty Lords:

"Yesterday arrived here the ship, the *Arms of Amsterdam*, which sailed from New Netherlands . . . on the 23d of September. They report that our people are in good heart and live in peace there. . . . They have purchased the Island of Manhattes from the Indians, for the value of sixty guilders. . . . They had all their grain sowed by the middle of May, and reaped by the middle of August. They send thence samples of summer grain; such as wheat, rye, barley, oats, buckwheat, canary seed, beans and flax.

"The cargo of the aforesaid ship is:
- 7246 beaver skins
- 178½ otter skins
- 675 otter skins
- 48 minck skins

> 36 wild cat skins
> 33 mincks
> 34 rat skins

"Considerable oak timber and hickory. Herewith, High and Mighty Lords, be commended to the mercy of the Almighty.

"Your High Mightinesses' obedient,
"P. SCHAGEN.
"In Amsterdam, Nov. 5, A.D. 1626."

THE PATROON SYSTEM.

Such a report as this could not fail to encourage merchants to invest in the new trade. The company made good offers to men who would take or send out over fifty settlers. Many rich men accepted the offers of patroonships. They were given large strips of land, especially along the Hudson River. The patroons, as these land-holders were called, received not only the land, but large powers of government over them and all the people who settled upon them, and also rights for extensive trade. To take up his patroonship, the patroon sent out fifty settlers, under bonds as "servants," in much the same way as the great Virginia planters' servants were indented. This, of course, increased the population of the New Netherland.

To induce still more people to settle in their

province, the Dutch West India Company offered other inducements in land and privileges to those who would take or send out even five settlers.

THE GREAT SEAPORT OF THE HUDSON.

After a few years, the company ordered that all the trade of the province, including that of all the patroon estates, should go through the port of New Amsterdam. Up to that time Fort Orange had perhaps as much business as there was at Manhattan, but this new order started the growth which soon made the great commercial city at the mouth of the Hudson.

The religious liberty and the trade attracted people to New Amsterdam from many different countries of Europe. The large export business of the company and the patroons created need for other kinds of trade and gave work to many merchants, skilled mechanics and laborers. People who did not like the strict life of the religious colonies of New England also flocked to the liberal Dutch colony. Redemptioners from the South, who had worked out their "time," or found other ways to repay the money spent for their passage, came to New Netherland to raise tobacco, as they had learned to do in Virginia.

These people from many places, brought different languages and different customs to the Dutch colony, and especially to the capital. They made from the beginning what we call a cosmopolitan place—that is, a place filled with people from many countries. In 1643 eighteen languages were spoken in New Amsterdam. It was then a pretty country village, with shops and docks upon the southeasterly end, and mills and ship-yards were near them, to the eastward, while the centre and westerly part of the island for a mile or so above the fort was laid out in tobacco-fields, cornfields and orchards.

CHAPTER XIX.

THE DUTCH AND THE INDIANS.

From the first the Indians were friendly to the Dutch. The traders began by paying them for their furs in the shells made into wampum, which was the Indians' money, or in cloth, or in the pretty toys the savages liked best. Besides that, the Dutch dealt fairly with them in trade and in buying their land for settlements. The Hudson River Indians, who were powerful tribes, liked the Dutch better than they did the French, who had settled to the north of them. This was largely because the French settlers had taken up the quarrels of some of the St. Lawrence tribes, who were enemies to the nations of the Hudson and of the Great Lakes.

For many years the Iroquois were the most powerful enemies of the French Indians, as the Hurons and others were called. The Iroquois lived near the lakes of Central New York. Since their enemies had white friends, the Iroquois would have white friends, too; and they turned with good-will toward the Dutch, taking them a large peltry trade, which the French desired and tried hard to get. Yet some Indians in New Netherland were not so friendly.

INDIAN TROUBLES.

The first troubles the Dutch had were mostly with the tribes of the region near what is now Jersey City. Their hostility spread to the Manhattan tribes, and sometimes up the river and among the Long Island natives. Each patroon kept the farmers, tobacco raisers and Indian traders of his estate far from any other. Each wanted to extend his own influence as much as he could among the Indians near his plantation. By treating the Indians as friendly and as familiarly as possible, each one tried to get more from them than his neighbor could get. This made the Indians jealous of each other and of the treatment they received from the different Dutch traders. The old saying that "familiarity breeds contempt," seems to be true in this case. The Indians lost all fear and respect for the Dutch farmers. When the farmers' cows strayed into the unfenced fields of corn, planted and owned by the Indians on the island, the Indians attacked the settlers, killing them and burning their houses. The farmers then realized how foolish they had been to place their houses so far apart that they lost each other's protection. Fort Amsterdam had been neglected until it was a poor defense. Many thought that the director was to blame for all the trouble. Eight colonists formed a sort of committee of complaint, and wrote to the home government:

" . . . We, poor inhabitants of New Netherlands, were, here in the spring, pursued by these wild heathens and barbarous savages with fire and sword; daily, in our houses and fields, have they cruelly murdered men and women, and with hatchets and tomahawks struck little children dead in their parents' arms or before their doors, or carried them away into bondage; the houses and grain barracks are burnt, with the produce; cattle of all descriptions are slain and destroyed. Such as remain must perish this approaching winter, for the want of fodder.

"Almost every place is abandoned. We, wretched people, must skulk, with wives and little ones that still survive, in poverty together, in and around the fort at the Manahatas, where we are not safe, even for an hour. . . . We are all here, from the smallest to the greatest, . . . wholly powerless. The enemy meets with scarce any resistance. The garrison (of the fort) consists of but about fifty or sixty soldiers, unprovided with ammunition. Fort Amsterdam, utterly defenceless, stands open to the enemy night and day." The eight then said that if prompt assistance did not come from the Dutch government, they would be obliged to call in aid from the New England colonies, and that the English probably would demand a share of the New Netherland trade in return for any help.

The fear of losing the valuable trade of the colony aroused the government in Holland. It called the company to account for this condition of things. The company said that the colonists brought much of the trouble upon themselves by living so far apart, by selling guns to the Indians, by allowing "free-traders"—men who did not belong to the company—to sail up the Hudson, and trade off guns and shot for furs. The company said that they were poor, and that they needed the aid of the Dutch government to keep the free-traders out of the province. If the government would aid them, they could promise to make things better for the colonists. They sent out instructions to the settlers to repair the fort, to live closer together, and to treat all the Indians alike. They tried to encourage the raising of tobacco, and told the settlers they could buy negroes at a fair price. In spite of these promises, the condition of affairs did not much improve. The directors, who were sent out from Holland to act as governors, seemed bent on having an easy life, and upon making as much money for themselves as they could.

ENGLISH NEIGHBORS.

The colonists of New England, by this time, were gradually spreading out through Connecticut, toward the New Netherland, and making settlements on Long Island. A story is told of an English ship, which appeared before Fort Amsterdam one day. The captain sent an invitation to Governor Van Twiller and his officers to come on board for a sort of banquet. Van Twiller went, and treated the Englishman in a friendly way. After staying six or seven days before the fort, the Englishman was allowed to go up the river, and carried on a large trade with the Indians before some of the indignant Dutch traders could induce the director to order him out of the river.

Wouter Van Twiller proved a poor governor. Kieft, his successor, was better in some ways, but stirred up the Indians into a revolt that did a great deal of harm to the Dutch settlements. Much as the Indians disliked Kieft, the Dutch settlers disliked him more. He treated them harshly, and would not allow them to appeal from his decisions to the government at home.

DIRECTOR STUYVESANT, 1647-1664.

The people of New Netherland put great hopes upon the new governor, Peter Stuyvesant. Some one wrote home, soon after the arrival of this new governor: "Mynheer Stuyvesant introduces here a thorough reform." According to Stuyvesant's own account, there was need of it. New Amsterdam was in a terrible condition.

"The people are without discipline, and approaching the savage state," he wrote. "A fourth part of the city of New Amsterdam consists of rumshops and houses where nothing can be had but beer and tobacco." Stuyvesant appears to have done his best, but that was not enough to save the settlement from passing out of the hands of the Dutch into those of the English.

ENGLAND'S CLAIM.

For many years English people had been looking on, while the Dutch settlement between New England and Virginia grew larger and richer. They claimed that the region belonged to England by virtue of Cabot's discovery. They were glad to see that affairs did not go smoothly under the Dutch company, and to hear that the company had not money enough to keep up a strong defense of the colony. So the English waited for the time when a well-aimed blow from them might strike down the Dutch power in New Netherlands, and secure the prize for themselves. There were two chief reasons why the English wanted the region about the Hudson: First, because New Amsterdam, the trading settlement at the mouth of the Hudson River, commanded one of the finest harbors in the world. Second, because, in order to carry out certain regulations about their commerce with the colonies, which ordered all of them to trade only with English merchants, they felt it necessary to close this Dutch market, with its strong temptations.

In 1664, during a war between the English and the Dutch in Europe, the English saw that their time had come to take possession of "the doorway to North America." Charles II. gave the whole region to his brother, James, Duke of York and Albany, and James sent Colonel Nichols across the Atlantic, to knock at the doorway, with four ships and 420 soldiers. New Amsterdam then had about 1,500 people, a stone fort and twenty cannon. Director Stuyvesant was ready to fight and to lead a resistance. But there were no men to follow. The colonists were willing to be taken under English government. So Stuyvesant surrendered without a fight.

THE CONQUEST, 1664.

The duke's lieutenant-governor, Colonel Nichols, took possession of all the territory claimed by the Dutch as the province of New York. That at first included what we call New Jersey. New Amsterdam became the town of New York. The fort was named Fort James. Fort Orange, on the Hudson, was called Albany. Other places received English names in the same way. Nothing was done violently. Much care was shown for the "Dutchmen," as all but the English in this cosmopolitan colony were called. They were still kept in public offices, although in name the government and the laws were made English. The every-day language and customs of the people were changed but little at first. Nichols offered religious freedom and every inducement possible to keep the settlers in the province and to tempt more to come. Within a few years many came from the other colonies and from the mother-country. The old towns grew rapidly and new ones were planted in many places.

You have seen the Dutch fur-trading post on Manhattan Island grow into a large English town. Here is a part of the first description of New York that was ever printed in the English language. It pictures the town and the whole province as they were in 1670.

"New York is built mostly of brick and stone, and covered with red and black tile, and the land being high, it gives at a distance a pleasing aspect to the spectators."

LONG ISLAND.

Next to Manhattan Island, the most important part of New York was Long Island. An old writer said:

"Long Island, the west end of which lies south-

New Amsterdam in 1673.

ward of New York, runs eastward above one hundred miles and is in some places eight, in some twelve, in some fourteen miles broad. It is inhabited from one end to the other. On the west end are four or five Dutch towns, the rest being all English, to the number of twelve, besides villages and farm houses. The island is most of it of a very good soil, and very natural for all sorts of English grain, which they sow and have very good increase of, besides all other fruits and herbs common in England, as also tobacco, hemp, flax, pumpkins and melons. The fruits natural to the island are mulberries, persimmons, grapes great and small, huckleberries, cranberries, plums of several sorts, raspberries and strawberries, of which last is such abundance in June that the fields and woods are dyed red. The island is plenti-

NEW AMSTERDAM IN 1673.

fully stored with all sorts of English cattle, horses, hogs, sheep, goats, . . . which they can both raise and maintain by reason of the large and spacious meadows or marshes wherewith it is furnished; the island likewise producing excellent English grass, which they sometimes mow twice a year."

Such an island as this was naturally attractive to the English people in the Connecticut colonies as well as to those in New York near its western end. Vessels from New York sailed through Long Island Sound on their way to New England, to trade. Ships from Boston and other Massachusetts ports sailed through the same sound to trade along the banks of the Hudson River. This brought about business and social ties between Boston and New York, even while it was New Amsterdam.

RETURN TO DUTCH RULE, 1673-1674.

The English rule was broken for about a year, when, in the war of England and Holland, it was taken by a Dutch admiral in 1673. You can see by the picture how large the seaport on Manhattan had grown by that time.

Peace was declared before Holland knew that the province had been retaken, and in the treaty the Dutch government yielded to England all claims in North America. The Dutch had done all the pioneering for New York. Even the important relations with Indians were made successful largely by following the best policy of the early Dutchmen.

NEW JERSEY AND DELAWARE.

What we know as New Jersey and Delaware were settled by Dutch people, Swedes and English Quakers. To the land in Delaware and the advantages of the Delaware River and Bay, both the Dutch and English made claims. The Dutch met with success until they were overshadowed by the Swedish colonists who came to make a new Sweden in America. Prosperous towns of thrifty, contented Swedes were growing up, when the Dutch, gathering force once more, overthrew their settlements. Then with New Amsterdam and New Netherlands, this region passed into the control of the Duke of York. In 1682 Penn secured a grant of it, and after that it was known as the "lower counties" of Pennsylvania until 1703. Then Delaware became a separate, though small and unimportant, colony.

CHAPTER XX.

THE PROVINCE OF PENN'S WOODS.

"PHILADELPHIA is at last laid out, to the general content of those here." These words were in a letter written in 1683 to Quakers in England by William Penn.

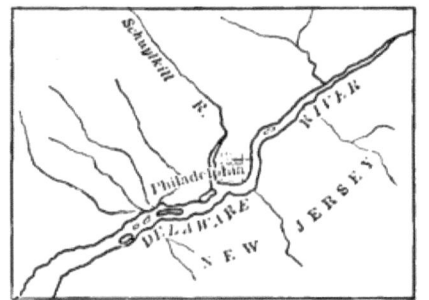

You know that Philadelphia is a large city in the southeastern part of Pennsylvania. I wonder if you have ever heard it called the Quaker City. Its settlers were members of the Society of Friends, who were commonly called Quakers. First, you will want to know who they were, and what their name meant. You remember that the Pilgrims who came to Plymouth, and the Puritans who came to Massachusetts Bay, were people who were not satisfied with the Church of England. They wanted simpler forms and more preaching. The Quakers were English people who wanted still more simple life, with peace and good will toward everyone. Some of their manners growing out of these ideas, seemed very odd to the rest of the world. In England they were so disliked that the Quakers were persecuted even more than any of the Puritans had been. They had a very hard time; but they were often saved from much harder times by a certain young man of whom Charles II. was fond, and whose father was the famous Admiral Penn. You all know his name—William Penn. He had many friends at the royal court, but handsome young Penn did not care for the gay life he might lead with these friends nearly so much as he cared to work for the Quakers and their belief.

THE QUAKER BELIEFS AND CUSTOMS.

Quakers believed that a person's ability to preach came not alone through education, but as a direct gift from God; and they felt that a power which came so freely ought to be given freely. So they had no regular and paid minister; every man or woman who attended a Quaker meeting might have words to speak. When they gathered all were quiet until some one felt moved to give a special message. Sometimes the silence was broken by earnest, strong appeals; at other times the silence was unbroken, yet they felt all had been worshiping in the true way.

In England often their meetings were interrupted by the entrance of government officers, who arrested their leaders, and sometimes all the people there.

George Fox, the first Quaker in England, and one who had many followers, was jeered at, and beaten by cruel mobs. "Reviled as a fanatic, and denounced as an impostor, yet he traveled from place to place, sometimes driven forth to sleep under haystacks; sometimes imprisoned as a disturber of the peace." Penn was arrested in the same way.

The Quakers could be recognized everywhere by their simplicity in dress. The men refused to lift their hats to anyone whom they met. They said God had created all men equal, and they would remove their hats only in their meeting-houses, in God's presence.

To carry out many of their beliefs, Quakers were obliged to break laws, and to seem disrespectful to men in authority. In holding their meetings they broke the same laws as the Pilgrims. They refused to take any oaths to support the government, or the king, because the Bible says, "swear not at all."

They would not take off their hats, even in the presence of the king. They felt there ought to be no paid ministers, and so they refused to pay taxes for the support of the English Church. In these ways they seemed to be disobedient and disrespectful, and their enemies had a chance to accuse them of other beliefs and evil designs.

These beliefs would not do any harm, or cause any uneasiness, in a state where all felt and acted alike. For that reason George Fox and William Penn spent much thought and time to establish a new home for the Friends of all the world. Some Quakers had already gone to the different colonies in the New World—to New England, where they were treated harshly in Massachusetts, but welcomed in Rhode Island. Others made settlements of their own near the Puritans and Churchmen in the colony of East Jersey. Still others started a colony of their own in West Jersey, near the Swedes and Dutch of the Delaware.

WILLIAM PENN.

Penn was interested in all of these settlements; but, after a time, he asked his friend, King Charles II., for a grant of land in America, to pay a debt due his father, Admiral Penn. This he wanted for a large colony, to be entirely settled and governed by Friends. It was to be a refuge for the persecuted Quakers from all parts of Europe. The king gave the grant in 1681. He named the great wooded tract Pennsylvania, or Penn's forest. William Penn wished another name, but his majesty insisted, because, he said, of his great admiration for Admiral Penn.

"After many waitings and watchings," William wrote to a friend, "this day my country was confirmed to me under the great seal of England. . . . Thou mayst communicate my grant to friends, and expect shortly my proposals."

Besides being an earnest Friend, ready and able to preach and write, William Penn was a careful business man. He deserved the title of a "Thrifty Gentleman of Pennsylvania." The land that had thus been given him in place of the money owed his father was to be his means of livelihood as well as a home for the Quakers. The proposals which he mentioned in the letter were about the terms on which land might be bought and occupied. He naturally felt that he must have some money return for his land. He offered 100 acres for £2 ($10) and a small yearly rent to be paid to him as proprietor, after the settlers were well established in their new homes. Meanwhile they must pay a fair price to any Indians who were in possession of the particular acres they wanted. From the first Penn treated the Indians fairly and became stanch friends with them. This was especially wise for the Quakers, for they did not believe in fighting, and would have been wholly unprotected and in danger if the Indians had been their enemies. The settlers who came out from England to take up land in Pennsylvania carried out Penn's instructions to make fair purchases from the Indians. Here is the account of a sale which gives you an idea of the prices paid. "Christian, the Indian, lord and owner of all the land between St. Jones and Duck Creek" sold and gave up claim "to John Brinkloe, planter, 600 acres woodland together with the marshes and creek." The pay was ten bottles of drink, four double handfuls of powder and four of shot and three match-coats — coats made of coarse goods called match-cloth.

A great emigration to Pennsylvania began in 1681. Most of the people were Quakers. Besides English people there were Swedes, Finns, Dutch, Scotch-Irish and Germans. These made many new settlements. Some of the newcomers joined settlements that had already been begun before the land was given to Penn. The principal settlement was Philadelphia, the "Quaker City," which Penn planned.

PHILADELPHIA.

Penn did not go out to Pennsylvania in 1681, but sent his instructions over by men called commissioners. In these orders Penn told the men to have the rivers and creeks sounded, and the shores explored in order to find a place high, dry and healthy with a good harbor. On this place there was to be built "a great town," Philadelphia. The streets were to be laid out in a regular way from the water's edge back into the country. Many of these streets were to be named for trees common in the country, such as Chestnut, Walnut and Spruce. From the very first a market place was provided for; "let the place for the store-house be on the middle of the key (quay), which will serve for market and store-house too." Among the instructions was this one about Penn's own house. "Pitch upon the very middle of the plot where the town or line of houses is to be laid . . . facing the harbor and great river for the situation of my house; yet let it not be one tenth part." One tenth was the amount he was allowed to have in common with others, but he said that a thirtieth part would do. Room was to be left about the houses for gardens and orchards, so as to add beauty to the town.

When William Penn came in the ship *Welcome* in 1682, he found the site chosen for Philadelphia on the narrow peninsula, between the Delaware and Schuykill Rivers. Look for it in the geography, and get from a guide-book a map of the city of Philadelphia. That will show you how the streets run down to the river bank. After Penn's arrival preparations went on rapidly. The laws made for all the settlements were so just and favorable that many more people were attracted to Pennsylvania, and of these many settled in Philadelphia. "In three years from its founding Philadelphia had gained more than New York City had done in half a century." In the year of Penn's arrival, and during the two following years, ships with immigrants arrived from London, Bristol, Ireland, Wales, Holland and Germany; for the "good news spread abroad that William Penn, the Quaker, had opened an asylum to the good and the oppressed of every nation."

Penn himself sent the praise of his country back to Europe. "The air," he said, "is sweet and clear, the heavens serene like the south parts of France, rarely overcast." He described the natural products of the country, especially the trees, valuable both for wood and fruit. "The fruits that I find in the woods are white and black mulberry, chestnut, walnut, plumbs and strawberries, cranberries, hurtleberries, and grapes of divers sortes."

"Here also are peaches, and very good and in great quantities; not an Indian plantation without them, but whether naturally here at first I know not; however, one may have bushels for little." He told them that farming and care enabled them to raise in this new country "wheat, barley, oats, rye, pease, beans, squashes, pumpkins, watermelons and all herbs and roots that our gardens in England usually bring forth." Of the fowl to be found in Pennsylvania, what most impressed Penn were the wild turkeys, which he said were forty and fifty pounds in weight. Of fish, the oysters pleased him especially, for he said some were six inches long.

Among the colonists who came in response to Penn's inducements were men of many trades and professions, but most of them were farmers, tradesmen or mechanics. Some of them were scholars who had studied at college, but most were men of little education. These were all interested in having their children taught, and the schools in Philadelphia were good even in the earliest years. One of the studies in each school was the laws of the colony.

DEALINGS WITH THE NATIVES.

The Indians especially felt themselves so well treated that they gave no cause for alarm. They showed, on the other hand, positive and frequent signs of friendliness. The settlers always bought their land fairly, and dealt seriously with them. Penn said, in warning the colonists against offending the Indians, "Be grave; they love not to be smiled upon." The Iroquois Indians called Penn Onas, and the Delawares called him Miquon. Both of these names mean quill or pen, so you see they merely translated his name into their own language. Perhaps the name seemed even more full of meaning to them because he had written letters to them and they had seen him sign treaties with their chiefs.

PENN'S TROUBLES.

William Penn's life, however, did not continue peaceful or prosperous. He had shown business skill and thrift as well as generosity in disposing of his land. When the rents became due the people did not act as generously or honestly, for they refused to pay them. His presence was needed in England, where even more serious enemies were working against him. His position as proprietor of Pennsylvania became an extremely difficult one. Once more he left his affairs in the colony to a commissioner or agent and went back to England. One letter to this agent reads: "Use thy utmost endeavors in the first place to receive all that is due to me. Get in quit-rents, and sell land according to my instructions; look carefully after all fines . . . that shall belong to me as proprietor and chief governor. Penn had need of this money, for as he said "Pennsylvania has been a dear Pennsylvania to me all over."

In 1688 the people of Philadelphia were filled with a groundless fear of an Indian outbreak, and they used the occasion to add to the feeling in England against Penn as proprietor and governor. So in 1692 the government was taken from Penn, and his colony was made a royal province.

The land still unsold remained in the hands of Penn, and later his family received money from its sale. Yet when Penn himself died, in 1718, he was almost bankrupt. Though his last days were sad, he had left behind him a beautiful, great city which was to be very important, not only in the history of his colony but of all the colonies during the years of the Revolutionary war period. But that was long after the pioneer days were passed.

New Century Copy-Books.

INTERMEDIAL SYSTEM PENMANSHIP. COMMON-SENSE METHOD. ON THE NATURAL SLANT OF 75 DEGREES.

DISTINCTIVE FEATURES:

1. The Intermedial Slant.
2. Round Hand and Minimum Shade.
3. Maximum of Legibility combined with Grace and Beauty of Script forms.
4. Facility of Execution.
5. Pictures, Illustrating Copies.
6. Significant Copy Sentences.

WHAT EDUCATORS SAY:

G. A. Booth, Ph. B., Hillhouse High School, New Haven, Conn. — "It gives me much pleasure to endorse your system of penmanship. It has long been my private opinion that the vertical writing would not satisfy business demands, and that a compromise must be effected. I believe that you have solved the problem."

J. M. Adams, Teacher of Penmanship, Ogden, Utah. — "Your system of copy-books is the 'happy medium' between the two extremes, and when taught from first grade to high school will, in my opinion, be a great improvement on any system yet produced."

Ella T. Heffron, Supervisor Penmanship, Utica, N. Y. — "I am much pleased with all the books. I feel sure the system will be a great help in securing better results in writing."

Lyman D. Smith, Supervisor Penmanship, Hartford, Conn. — "Your Copy-Books, which we have been using in all our classes, give great satisfaction. Every teacher is loud in praise of the style of the writing and the character of the matter for practice. I have never seen pupils so carried away with new copy-books in all my teaching."

WHAT BUSINESS MEN SAY:

W. C. Vosburgh Mfg. Company, Limited, F. L. Strickland, Treas., Brooklyn, N. Y. — "An examination of the penmanship of correspondence, etc., sent to this house, shows that most of it is on a 75 degree slant."

London and Lancashire Fire Insurance Co., N. Y. City, F. E. Shaw, Agency Supt. — "We beg to say that we find the majority of our staff write at an angle between 70 and 80 degrees."

Wm. A. Kremer, Secretary, German-American Insurance Co., New York. — "We beg to say that a large number of our force write at an angle of 75 degrees, very few, indeed, exceeding the 80 or less than the 70. We find that the vertical writers are quite slow."

	PER DOZ.
Illustrated Writing Primer	$0.72
Short Course, Nos. 1-2-3-4	.72
Regular Course, Nos. 1-2-3-4-5-6-7-8	.96

Liberal Discount to Schools.

THE IDEAL SYSTEM OF WRITING FOR AMERICAN SCHOOLS.

THE MORSE COMPANY...PUBLISHERS,

MAIN OFFICE: 96 FIFTH AVE., NEW YORK.

CHICAGO: FISHER BUILDING.   BOSTON: 36 BROMFIELD ST.

FAIRY TALE AND FABLE.

BY

JOHN G. THOMPSON,
PRIN. STATE NORMAL SCHOOL, FITCHBURG, MASS.

THOS. E. THOMPSON,
SUPERINTENDENT SCHOOLS, LEOMINSTER, MASS.

THE PIONEER BOOK OF HIGH ART IN PRIMARY READING.

Illustrated with Reproductions from Great Artists—Landseer, Rosa Bonheur, Von Bremen, Troyon, and others.

Mailing Price 42 Cents. Liberal Discount to Schools.

Rev. A. E. Winship, Editor "Journal of Education," Boston.—"This is one of the great first readers, of which two or three others have appeared this year, none of which is better than this. It is certainly clear that the first readers will be on a new line hereafter. The editor knows this book in use, and delights to testify to its working qualities. *The masterpieces of art have never before appeared in any first reader.* There are seventeen full-page reproductions of the most appropriate works of the great masters. On the first page are given 200 words with which the children are supposed to have been made familiar through blackboard work before taking the book."

F. Lilian Taylor, Prin. Training School, Galesburg, Ill.—"I think 'Fairy Tale and Fable' an excellent book, and propose very soon to send an order."

E. G. Ward, Ass't Supt. of Instruction, Brooklyn, N. Y., Public Schools.—"A most exquisite book in every respect."

Sarah L. Arnold, Supervisor of Schools, Boston, Mass.—"I am delighted with 'Fairy Tale and Fable.' I hope the book will have the wide sale it deserves."

Dr. C. H. Levermore, Pres. Adelphi College, Brooklyn, N. Y.—"We have examined carefully 'Fairy Tale and Fable,' and all endorse it most heartily. We shall order it soon."

Gratia L. Rice, Supervisor of Drawing, Buffalo Schools.—"It is my idea of an artistic school-book. May success attend it."

C. N. Kendall, Supt. Schools, New Haven, Conn.—"Our Board, at its last meeting, put on our list 'Fairy Tale and Fable' by Thompson. We shall want a number of this book during the year."

Karl Mathie, Supt. Schools, Wausau, Wis.—"Send us forty more of your 'incomparable' 'Fairy Tale and Fable.'"

Adopted and in general use in New York City, Boston, Mass., Brooklyn, N. Y., Newark, N. J., Philadelphia, Pa., Denver, Col., Jersey City, N. J., New Haven, Conn., Worcester, Mass., Cook County, Ill., Morgantown, N. C., Dallas, Tex., Bridgeport, Conn., Wausau, Wis., Waukegan, Ill., Sioux City, Ia., and in hundreds of other places.

THE MORSE COMPANY...PUBLISHERS,
MAIN OFFICE: 96 FIFTH AVE., NEW YORK.

CHICAGO OFFICE: FISHER BUILDING.   BOSTON OFFICE: 36 BROMFIELD ST.

THE PHONETIC READER.

BY CHARLES W. DEANE, PH. D.,
SUPT. OF SCHOOLS, BRIDGEPORT, CONN.

EASY AND RAPID METHOD FOR TEACHING READING.
HIGH-ART ILLUSTRATIONS, CHOICE LITERATURE.
RESULTS FROM USE COMMEND THIS BOOK.

Mailing Price 40 Cents.   Liberal Discount to Schools.

 Orville T. Bright, Supt. Schools, Cook Co., Ill.—"I wish to say that I think the book a genuine contribution to the teaching of little children. I am delighted with it. You have done what nobody else has—placed the subject of phonics in its proper relation to the literature that should enter into a first reader. In other words, whoever reads this book through will have uppermost in his mind, as it should be, the reading lessons, that is the substance of the lessons, not the manner of presenting them. I believe you have handled the subject of phonics better than anybody else in cold print. The best part of it all is, as I have indicated, that it is subordinate. As a teacher of long experience, and a man whose whole interest in life is connected with schools, I wish to thank you for having written the book."

 W. A. McCord, County Supt., Polk Co., Des Moines., Ia.—"I find that Deane's 'Phonetic Reader' meets my ideas to a dot."

 The editor of one of the large educational companies writes: "'The Phonetic Reader' is the best thing of its kind yet published. Mr. Deane has surely used the best there is in all other systems, and in the word and sentence method."

 Cyrus Boger, Supt. Schools, Lebanon, Pa.—"In Deane's 'Phonetic Reader' the truth that the child must first learn to read before it can read to learn, is fully recognized. The method is most excellent, and the reproductions from great artists emphasize the fact that a child's book ought to contain the best in art as well as in literature."

 H. E. Bennett, Principal, Fernandina, Fla.—"Your primary books are the finest I have ever seen. Much credit is due you for putting such works of art in the hands of children. Our primary teachers are delighted with them, especially Deane's 'Phonetic Reader.'"

 Lewis E. Funnell, Prin. Stamford Public Schools, Stamford, Conn.—"I am very much pleased with Deane's 'Phonetic Reader.' Its plan is in perfect harmony with the correct ideas of teaching reading."

 Chas. Eldred Shelton, Supt. City Schools, Burlington, Ia.—"This is an excellent piece of text-book work. A gem in its line."

 Chas. Emerson, County Supt., Creston, Ia.—"It is the best of the kind I ever saw."

THE MORSE COMPANY...PUBLISHERS,
MAIN OFFICE: 96 FIFTH AVE., NEW YORK.

CHICAGO OFFICE: FISHER BUILDING. BOSTON OFFICE: 36 BROMFIELD ST.

NEW CENTURY DEVELOPMENT MAPS.

DESIGNED BY H. A. MACGOWAN,
PRINCIPAL HIGH SCHOOL, MARBLEHEAD, MASS.

AN ENTIRELY NEW AS WELL AS ELABORATE SERIES OF MAPS IN OUTLINE.

For use in Elementary and Secondary Schools for representing the innumerable features that may be expressed graphically of **Physical, Political, Mathematical and Descriptive Geography, History, Meteorology, Geology and Statistics.**

PRONOUNCED BY PRACTICAL EDUCATORS
TO BE THE BEST AND MOST ECONOMICAL.

READY.

North America,	Single Map,	30	Cents per Block.
South America,	Single Map,	30	" " "
Europe,	Double Map,	30	" " "
Asia,	Double Map,	30	" " "
Africa,	Single Map,	30	" " "
United States,	Double Map,	30	" " "
Middle Atlantic States,	Single Map,	30	" " "
The World on the Mercator Projection,	Single Map,	30	" " "
British Isles,	Single Map,	30	" " "
Mediterranean Countries,	Double Map,	30	" " "
New England,	Single Map,	30	" " "
Central States (eastern section),	Single Map,	30	" " "
Southern States (eastern section),	Single Map,	30	" " "
Pacific States (northern section),	Single Map,	30	" " "
Australia,	Double Map,	30	" " "

Richard E. Dodge, Associate Professor Natural Science, Teachers' College, New York City.—"The series of outline maps published by The Morse Company are a very valuable addition to the mechanical outfit for teaching the geographical distribution of peoples, climate, physical features, products, etc. The maps are printed on good paper, of a size to be readily inserted in note books, and are put up in blocks of fifty, each selling at thirty cents a block. They are cheap, clear and convenient, and are far better than any other outline maps, raised or plain, thus far examined."

THE MORSE COMPANY...PUBLISHERS,
MAIN OFFICE: 96 FIFTH AVE., NEW YORK.

CHICAGO OFFICE: FISHER BUILDING.   BOSTON OFFICE: 36 BROMFIELD ST.

HISTORICAL READER.

BY ALMA HOLMAN BURTON.

A PIONEER BOOK. COVERS AN UNBEATEN TRACK.
WITH 16 FULL-PAGE AUTHENTIC ILLUSTRATIONS.

12mo, Cloth, 75 Cents. Liberal Discount to Schools.

IN a History of the United States, the fate of the Indians is only an incident in the settlement of the country.

The theme of the historian is the white man; and so marvellous is the national drama, so dazzling are the achievements of the Puritan and Cavalier, that the Red Man has little more space in our annals than the primeval forest which once covered the continent.

The author has treated the subject of the Indians historically. A few chapters have been devoted to the early Colonial life, because the growth and development of the Puritan marks the decline and exile of the Algonquins.

For the study, in an attractive form, of the annals of the once proud race whose broken fragments still linger in the rays of the setting sun, this book seems eminently fitted, with its choice language, as a Supplementary Reader for the middle grades in all of our public schools.

TESTIMONIALS.

A. S. Draper, President University of Illinois.—"It is a fascinating contribution to New England literature, upon a subject which is admirably adapted for school work."

Wm. T. Harris, Commissioner, Bureau of Education, Washington, D. C.—"This is a most valuable book for school work on the subject of the Indians and Colonial times."

THE MORSE COMPANY...PUBLISHERS,
MAIN OFFICE: 96 FIFTH AVE., NEW YORK.

CHICAGO OFFICE: FISHER BUILDING.   BOSTON OFFICE: 36 BROMFIELD ST.

NATURE'S BYWAYS.

By NELLIE WALTON FORD.

Natural Science for Primary Pupils, beautifully illustrated by reproductions from Great Artists; Literature, a Juvenile Poem.

Mailing Price, 40c.   Liberal Discount to Schools.

B. M. Phelan, Prin. St. Paul Teachers' Training School.—Please send enclosed order for "Nature's Byways" for use in first grade. We have wanted a book of this kind for use in connection with our nature study, and I am glad you have succeeded in putting Miss Ford's lessons in so attractive a form.

Prof. M. V. O'Shea, School of Pedagogy, University of Buffalo, N. Y.—I am particularly pleased with "Nature's Byways." I have no hesitation in saying that it appears to be a delightful book, and most happily adapted for beginners in reading. The selections seem well chosen and admirably arranged. The book emphasizes the thought side in reading, and minimizes the attention which is given to purely formal drills upon words. The illustrations are especially to be praised. I feel certain that you have produced a *culture book* for children. *Mechanically it is perfect.*

Richard C. Boone, Prin. Michigan State Normal School, Ypsilanti, Mich.—I have examined "Nature's Byways" with great satisfaction. Among all books on natural science for children, especially for the younger children, this seems to me one of the sanest and most practical. It is admirable in its subject matter and not less satisfactory in its arrangement. I congratulate you and the author upon so great success in presenting the natural sciences to children.

Mary F. Hall, Primary Supervisor, Public Schools, Milwaukee, Wis.—Of all the books I have seen that are based on the idea of relating the early reading lessons to the lessons on nature objects, "Nature's Byways" seems the most widely useful to all teachers, both in its selection and treatment of matter. The high art illustrations, as well as its general artistic features, *make the book one of unusual merit.*

Rev. A. E. Winship, Editor "Journal of Education."—This charmingly illustrated book is admirably adapted to interest young children in natural science. It is, in a sense, a graded reader, stimulating to nature study. The language chosen is almost classical in its purity and simplicity. Each lesson becomes a model for the young pupil to follow in writing his own description of leaves, flowers, fruits, animals and things in nature. The reproductions of the great artists are so accurately described in the text, as to become real lessons in art.

Anna M. Nolte, Kindergartner, Hardy School, Duluth, Minn.—I heartily recommend "Nature's Byways" for its simplicity, its artistic nature, and clear, positive style of expressing thought, helping the child to understand nature aright.

Mary Louise Eastman, Prin. Primary Dept., State Normal School, Cortland, N. Y.—We endorse "Nature's Byways" most heartily, and, as proof, we have ordered a number of copies.

Marietta Mathews, Primary Dept., Public Schools, Worcester, Mass.—The beautiful book, "Nature's Byways," received. All the teachers think it charming.

Marietta L. Pierce, Prin. Primary Dept., Normal School, Mankato, Minn.—I am exceedingly well pleased with "Nature's Byways." It is a gem as to style, and the sentences, to my judgment, are particularly well adapted to first grade work. I am delighted with the illustrations, especially the reproduction from great artists. I believe the book will be of great value in any primary school. We shall use it in our school.

ADOPTED IN NEW YORK CITY, BROOKLYN, NEWARK, JERSEY CITY, BUFFALO, PHILADELPHIA, BOSTON, CHICAGO, ETC.

The Universal Verdict is that "Nature's Byways" is the Best Natural Science Reader in print.

THE MORSE COMPANY, PUBLISHERS.

MAIN OFFICE: 96 FIFTH AVENUE, NEW YORK.

CHICAGO OFFICE: FISHER BUILDING.   BOSTON OFFICE: 36 BROMFIELD ST.

SOME NEW AND ATTRACTIVE BOOKS.

STANDARD SCHOOL ALGEBRA. By Geo. E. Atwood. A book by a practical teacher, who is recognized as an expert in teaching Algebra. An epoch book in mathematics. Mailing price, $1.20.

PHONETIC READER. By Chas. W. Deane, Ph. D. Easy and Rapid Method for Teaching Reading. High Art Illustrations. Choice Literature. Mailing price, 40 cents.

THOMPSON'S FAIRY TALE AND FABLE. A Pioneer Book of High Art in Primary Reading. Illustrated with Reproductions from Great Artists. Landseer, Rosa Bonheur, Van Marcke, Troyon, and others. Mailing price, 40 cents.

NATURE'S BYWAYS. By Nellie Walton Ford. Natural Science for Primary Pupils; beautifully illustrated by Reproductions from Great Artists; Literature, a Juvenile Poem. Mailing price, 40 cents.

MORSE SPELLER. By Samuel T. Dutton, Supt. of Schools, Brookline, Mass. Correlation of spelling with History, Geography, Science, etc. Suited for eight grades. Mailing price, cloth, 30 cents; boards, 24 cents. Part I., 15 cents; Part II., 20 cents.

GEMS OF GERMAN LITERATURE. A choice selection of German Verse from best authors, in German, for practical school work. Mailing price, 40 cents.

A NATURE CALENDAR. By Thomas E. Thompson. Indispensable Memorandum-book for students of Botany and Nature. English and Scientific names of Flowers, Trees, Birds, etc., with space for data covering four years. Mailing price, 30 cents.

NEW CENTURY DEVELOPMENT MAPS. Best in use. Price one-half that of similar maps. Utility greater. In blocks of 50 outline Maps. Two sizes. Mailing price, 40 cents per block.

EASY EXPERIMENTS IN PHYSICS. By Preston Smith, State Normal School, Fitchburg, Mass. The Work of a Practical Instructor. Original in Arrangement. Simple in Method. A Book for Solid Foundation Work. Mailing price, 50 cents.

HISTORICAL READER. By Alma Holman Burton. The Story of the Indians of New England. With sixteen full-page authentic illustrations. A pioneer book. Covers an unbeaten track. A valuable reader for all middle grades. Full of accurate information of Colonial days. Mailing price, 66 cents.

NEW CENTURY COPY BOOKS. Intermedial System. Extremes meet in this system. Method represents average of business-house writing. Primer and four books, short course, 72 cents per dozen. Eight books, regular course, 96 cents per dozen.

NEW CENTURY BUSY WORK. What the Primary Teachers Have Been Looking For. Entirely New. 17 Distinct different sets in boxes. High Art Illustrations. Mailing prices, 15c., 20c., 25c.

LIBERAL DISCOUNT TO SCHOOLS.
Many other Choice Books soon ready.

THE MORSE COMPANY, Publishers,
MAIN OFFICE: 96 FIFTH AVENUE, NEW YORK.

CHICAGO OFFICE: FISHER BUILDING.   BOSTON OFFICE: 36 BROMFIELD ST.

www.ingramcontent.com/pod-product-compliance
Lightning Source LLC
Chambersburg PA
CBHW031932230426
43672CB00010B/1904